CN-57

MW01195234

THIS IS YOUR **PASSBOOK**® FOR ...

OCCUPATIONAL HEALTH NURSING

NATIONAL LEARNING CORPORATION®
passbooks.com

PASSBOOK® SERIES

THE *PASSBOOK® SERIES* has been created to prepare applicants and candidates for the ultimate academic battlefield – the examination room.

At some time in our lives, each and every one of us may be required to take an examination – for validation, matriculation, admission, qualification, registration, certification, or licensure.

Based on the assumption that every applicant or candidate has met the basic formal educational standards, has taken the required number of courses, and read the necessary texts, the *PASSBOOK® SERIES* furnishes the one special preparation which may assure passing with confidence, instead of failing with insecurity. Examination questions – together with answers – are furnished as the basic vehicle for study so that the mysteries of the examination and its compounding difficulties may be eliminated or diminished by a sure method.

This book is meant to help you pass your examination provided that you qualify and are serious in your objective.

The entire field is reviewed through the huge store of content information which is succinctly presented through a provocative and challenging approach – the question-and-answer method.

A climate of success is established by furnishing the correct answers at the end of each test.

You soon learn to recognize types of questions, forms of questions, and patterns of questioning. You may even begin to anticipate expected outcomes.

You perceive that many questions are repeated or adapted so that you can gain acute insights, which may enable you to score many sure points.

You learn how to confront new questions, or types of questions, and to attack them confidently and work out the correct answers.

You note objectives and emphases, and recognize pitfalls and dangers, so that you may make positive educational adjustments.

Moreover, you are kept fully informed in relation to new concepts, methods, practices, and directions in the field.

You discover that you arre actually taking the examination all the time: you are preparing for the examination by "taking" an examination, not by reading extraneous and/or supererogatory textbooks.

In short, this PASSBOOK®, used directedly, should be an important factor in helping you to pass your test.

CERTIFIED NURSE EXAMINATION SERIES

NURSING EXAMINATION RESOURCES

A variety of tests and programs are available through a number of organizations that will aid and help prepare candidates for nursing certification:

AMERICAN NURSES CREDENTIALING CENTER (ANCC)

The American Nurses Credentialing Center (ANCC) is a subsidiary of the American Nurses' Association (ANA), and the largest nursing credentialing organization in the United States. The ANCC Commission on Certification offers approximately 40 examinations including advanced practice specialties for nurse practitioners and clinical nurse specialists.

Certification is a most important way for you to show that you are among the best in your field – an extra step for you and your career, a step *beyond* state licensing. It gives you recognition and status on a *national* basis.

ANCC certification exams are offered twice a year in May and October in paper-and-pencil format, and throughout the year as computer-based exams. All exams are multiple choice and cover knowledge, understanding and application of professional nursing practice and theory. The time allotted for both the paper-and-pencil and computer certification exams is 3 hours and 30 minutes.

Each exam is developed in cooperation with an individual Content Expert Panel (CEP) composed of experts representing specific areas of certification. These panels analyze the professional skills and abilities required and then define which content should be covered and how strongly emphasized. Test questions are written by certified nurses in their discipline and reviewed by the ANCC to ensure validity and quality.

Exams are scored on a scale, and will be reported as either "Pass" or "Fail." Those who fail the exam will receive diagnostic information for each area of the test. There is a minimum 90-day waiting period from the date of the failed exam for those looking to retake it. For those who pass the exam, a certificate, official identification card and pin will be sent. Certification is valid for five years.

For further information and application for admission to candidacy for certification, write to:

American Nurses Credentialing Center
8515 Georgia Ave., Suite 400
Silver Spring, MD 20910-3492

You can also contact the ANCC and receive further details regarding certification exams and registration by visiting its home on the Internet – www.nursecredentialing.org – or by phone (1-800-284-CERT). Test Content Outlines (TCO) for each exam can also be found on the ANCC website, detailing the format and content breakdown of the test as well as the content areas the examinee should be prepared for.

NATIONAL CERTIFICATION CORPORATION

NCC CERTIFICATION

NCC – the National Certification Corporation for the Obstetric, Gynecologic and Neonatal Nursing specialties – is an independent certification organization. NCC was established in 1975 as a non-profit corporation for the purpose of sponsoring a volunteer certification program.

BENEFITS OF CERTIFICATION

Certification serves as an added credential to attest to attainment of special knowledge beyond the basic nursing degree. Certification serves to maintain and promote quality nursing care by providing a mechanism to nurses to demonstrate their special knowledge in a specific nursing area.

Promotion of quality care through certification benefits not only the individual nurse and the profession of nursing, but the public as well. Certification documents to employers, professional colleagues and health team members that special knowledge has been achieved, provides for expanded career opportunities and advancement within the specialty of OGN nursing, and elevates the standards of the obstetric, gynecologic and neonatal nursing practice.

Certification granted by NCC is pursuant to a voluntary procedure intended solely to test for special knowledge.

NCC does not purport to license, to confer a right or privilege upon, nor otherwise to define qualifications of any person for nursing practice.

The significance of certification in any jurisdiction or institution is the responsibility of the candidate to determine. The candidate should contact the appropriate state board of nursing or institution.

EXAMINATION DEVELOPMENT

NCC selects educators and practitioners in both nursing and medicine who possess expertise in the specialty areas within the obstetric, gynecologic and neonatal nursing and related fields to serve on the test committees. Responsibilities of the test committees include coordination of overall development of certification examinations and development of materials to assist candidates to assess readiness to participate in the certification process.

EXAMINATION DESCRIPTION

Each of the examinations consists of 200 multiple-choice questions. Two forms of each examination are often given to provide the opportunity to perform statistical procedures which ensure added reliability to the total examination process. The examinations are offered only in English and are designed to test special knowledge.

The examinations are given once each in the morning and afternoon, Monday through Friday, at more than 100 test centers. Four hours are allotted for completion of the examination.

THE CERTIFICATION PROCESS

1. Applicants must complete and file a certification application and appropriate documentation and fees
2. An acknowledgment postcard is sent to each applicant when NCC receives the application
3. Eligibility to participate is determined
4. Applicant is notified of eligibility status and eligible candidate receives a Candidate Guide to NCC Certification (4 to 6 weeks from receipt of application)
5. Candidates will schedule their own appointment for an examination time and location, and must take the exam within a 90-day period from notification of eligibility
6. Test administration occurs
7. Examinations are scored and analyzed
8. Candidates receive score reports upon completion of computerized testing (not paper testing)
9. Candidates are notified of certification status, receive information about certification maintenance and are later issued formal certificates

REVIEW COURSES AND NCC

NCC does not sponsor or endorse any review courses or materials for the certification examinations, because to do so would be a conflict of interest.

NCC is not affiliated with and does not provide input or information for any review courses or materials that other organizations may offer.

NCC views certification as an evaluative process. Eligibility criteria have been established to identify a minimum level of preparation for the exams.

CANDIDATE GUIDE TO NCC CERTIFICATION

Each candidate determined eligible to participate in the NCC certification process will be sent a Guide to NCC Certification. These guides can also be found online at the NCC website (www.nccnet.org). The Candidate Guides contain:

*   General policies and procedures about the certification process
*   Competency Statements that serve as a role description for the specialty nurse
*   Expanded examination content outline
*   Bibliography of references
*   Sample questions to familiarize candidates with examination format (*These questions are not representative of exam content or difficulty level)

The Candidate Guide is not provided as study material, but to assist candidates in evaluating their own nursing practice as they prepare for the certification examination through identification of potential areas of strength and weakness.

SCORING OF EXAMINATIONS

Passing scores are determined based on a criterion-referenced system. Criterion passing scores are established by the NCC Board of Directors in conjunction with the NCC Test Committees using standard psychometric procedures.

Each question is statistically analyzed and evaluated with psychometric consultation, and scores are computed based on this evaluation.

Candidates who take the computerized form of the certification exam will receive their score reports upon completion of the exam. Those who take the paper/pencil exam will not receive their score reports for several weeks after administration.

NOTIFICATION AND AWARDING OF CERTIFICATION

Each candidate is notified of the success or failure to achieve certification. Successful candidates receive a formal certificate and will be able to use the initial RNC (Registered Nurse Certified) to indicate certification status.

Certification is awarded for a period of three years. Initial certification is effective from the date of notification to December 31 of the third full calendar year following notification. Subsequent periods of certification are subject to policies of the Certification Maintenance Program.

CERTIFICATION MAINTENANCE

The NCC Certification Maintenance Program allows the certified nurse to maintain NCC certification status.

Certification status must be maintained on an ongoing basis every three years through demonstration of approved continuing education or reexamination. Certification that is not maintained through the Certification Maintenance Program may only be regained by reexamination.

Specific information about the Certification Maintenance Program is provided to successful certification candidates and may also be obtained by contacting the NCC website (www.nccnet.org).

GENERAL POLICIES

All required practice experience/employment must have occurred while the applicant is/was a U.S. or Canadian RN. Graduate Nurse or Interim Permit status is acceptable, but must be indicated separately on the application form in addition to original licensure information.

NCC defines employment as practice in any of the following settings: direct patient care, educational institutions, administration or research.

When meeting educational requirements, all coursework, including that not directly related to specialty areas, thesis work and/or other program requirements must be completed at the time the application is filed.

It is the policy of NCC that no individual shall be excluded from the opportunity to participate in the NCC certification program on the basis of race, national origin, religion, sex, age or handicap.

All applications received are subject to the nonrefundable application fee ($250 paper/pencil; $300 computer).

Incomplete applications or applications submitted without appropriate fees will be returned and subject to all policies, fees and deadlines.

Applicants determined eligible (whether the candidate has been notified or not) and withdrawn will be subject to stated refund policies.

All NCC policies and requirements are subject to change without notice.

RETEST POLICIES

The NCC does not limit the number of times a candidate may retake the NCC Certification Examinations. Unsuccessful candidates who wish to be retested must reapply, submit all applicable fees and documentation, and re-establish eligibility.

<u>Eligibility:</u> All eligibility criteria of practice experience and/or educational preparation must be met by the time of application. It is the candidate's decision to choose the appropriate examination, based on the content outline, the individual's practice experience and NCC eligibility criteria.

<u>Forms:</u> All required forms must be submitted, and must include all requested information. If the forms are missing information, your application will be returned or you may be found ineligible to sit for the exam. Be sure the RN licensure information is completed. Be sure your documentation is signed by your supervisor or program director, with his/her title indicated, and the date the form is signed. Review your forms before you submit them.

<u>Fees and Refunds:</u> The proper fee must be submitted with your application or it will be returned.

For a current exam catalog containing current fees, terms, filing deadlines and exam dates, contact the NCC at www.nccnet.org, call (312) 951-0207 or fax at (312) 951-9475.

National Certification Corporation
PO Box 11082
Chicago, IL 60611-0082

CENTER FOR CERTIFICATION PREPARATION AND REVIEW

The Center for Certification Preparation and Review (CCPR) provides practice examinations developed by nurses and is intended to familiarize candidates with the content and feel of the real test. The CCPR practice examination identifies content areas of strength and weakness, provides examples of the type and format of questions that will appear on the examination, as well as information on how to focus additional study efforts.

The CCPR program consists of: study strategies, competency statements, content outline, 160-item examination, answer key and sample answer sheet, performance assessment grid, rationales for answers and cited references. Exams are available for inpatient obstetric, maternal newborn, neonatal intensive care and low-risk neonatal nursing, as well as neonatal nurse practitioner and women's health care nurse practitioner.

More information on ordering these practice exams can be found at www.ccprnet.org.

The National Certification Corporation (NCC), a not-for-profit organization that provides a national credentialing program for nurses, physicians and other licensed health care personnel, offers candidate guides for each of the NCC examinations. These candidate guides contain competency statements, detailed test outlines, sample questions, list of book/periodical references and all NCC policies related to the test administration process.

NCC guides are available in the following areas: inpatient obstetric, low-risk neonatal, maternal newborn and neonatal intensive care nursing, as well as neonatal nurse practitioner, telephone nursing practice, women's health care nurse practitioner, electronic fetal monitoring subspecialty examination, and menopause clinician. These guides, in addition to other information regarding testing, NCC publications and links to other organizations, are available online at www.nccnet.org.

RESOURCES FOR PRE-ADMISSION AND ACHIEVEMENT TESTS IN RN AND PN PROGRAMS

The National League for Nursing (NLN) offers a wide variety of examinations designed to aid students looking to further their education in the field of nursing. NLN pre-admission exams are reliable and valid predictors of student success in nursing programs, and NLN achievement tests allow educators to evaluate course or program objectives and to compare student performance to a national sample. The NLN also provides Diagnostic Readiness Tests, Critical Thinking and Comprehensive Nursing Achievement Exams and Acceleration Challenge Exams.

NLN exams can be ordered in paper form or e-mailed directly to you as online tests. The RN program includes tests in: basic nursing care, nursing care of children, maternity and child health nursing, nursing care of adults, psychiatric mental health and pharmacology in clinical nursing, baccalaureate achievement, physical assessment, community health nursing, comprehensive psychiatric nursing, heath and illness, anatomy and physiology, and microbiology.

NLN achievement tests also cover a PN program, which includes exams in: PN fundamentals, maternity infant, child health and adult health nursing, as well as mental health concepts and PN pharmacology.

NLN Pre-NCLEX Readiness Tests serve as practice and review for the NCLEX. Comprehensive Nursing Achievement, Critical Thinking and Diagnostic Readiness Tests are complementary to one another and help students prepare for nursing practice and to pass the NCLEX.

For in-depth information about the types of tests available, ordering, and additional NLN publications, including the NLN test catalog (available for download), visit www.nln.org.

HOW TO TAKE A TEST

You have studied long, hard and conscientiously.

With your official admission card in hand, and your heart pounding, you have been admitted to the examination room.

You note that there are several hundred other applicants in the examination room waiting to take the same test.

They all appear to be equally well prepared.

You know that nothing but your best effort will suffice. The "moment of truth" is at hand: you now have to demonstrate objectively, in writing, your knowledge of content and your understanding of subject matter.

You are fighting the most important battle of your life—to pass and/or score high on an examination which will determine your career and provide the economic basis for your livelihood.

What extra, special things should you know and should you do in taking the examination?

I. YOU MUST PASS AN EXAMINATION

A. WHAT EVERY CANDIDATE SHOULD KNOW

Examination applicants often ask us for help in preparing for the written test. What can I study in advance? What kinds of questions will be asked? How will the test be given? How will the papers be graded?

B. HOW ARE EXAMS DEVELOPED?

Examinations are carefully written by trained technicians who are specialists in the field known as "psychological measurement," in consultation with recognized authorities in the field of work that the test will cover. These experts recommend the subject matter areas or skills to be tested; only those knowledges or skills important to your success on the job are included. The most reliable books and source materials available are used as references. Together, the experts and technicians judge the difficulty level of the questions.

Test technicians know how to phrase questions so that the problem is clearly stated. Their ethics do not permit "trick" or "catch" questions. Questions may have been tried out on sample groups, or subjected to statistical analysis, to determine their usefulness.

Written tests are often used in combination with performance tests, ratings of training and experience, and oral interviews. All of these measures combine to form the best-known means of finding the right person for the right job.

II. HOW TO PASS THE WRITTEN TEST

A. BASIC STEPS

1) Study the announcement

How, then, can you know what subjects to study? Our best answer is: "Learn as much as possible about the class of positions for which you've applied." The exam will test the knowledge, skills and abilities needed to do the work.

Your most valuable source of information about the position you want is the official exam announcement. This announcement lists the training and experience qualifications. Check these standards and apply only if you come reasonably close to meeting them. Many jurisdictions preview the written test in the exam announcement by including a section called "Knowledge and Abilities Required," "Scope of the Examination," or some similar heading. Here you will find out specifically what fields will be tested.

2) Choose appropriate study materials

If the position for which you are applying is technical or advanced, you will read more advanced, specialized material. If you are already familiar with the basic principles of your field, elementary textbooks would waste your time. Concentrate on advanced textbooks and technical periodicals. Think through the concepts and review difficult problems in your field.

These are all general sources. You can get more ideas on your own initiative, following these leads. For example, training manuals and publications of the government agency which employs workers in your field can be useful, particularly for technical and professional positions. A letter or visit to the government department involved may result in more specific study suggestions, and certainly will provide you with a more definite idea of the exact nature of the position you are seeking.

3) Study this book!

III. KINDS OF TESTS

Tests are used for purposes other than measuring knowledge and ability to perform specified duties. For some positions, it is equally important to test ability to make adjustments to new situations or to profit from training. In others, basic mental abilities not dependent on information are essential. Questions which test these things may not appear as pertinent to the duties of the position as those which test for knowledge and information. Yet they are often highly important parts of a fair examination. For very general questions, it is almost impossible to help you direct your study efforts. What we can do is to point out some of the more common of these general abilities needed in public service positions and describe some typical questions.

1) General information

Broad, general information has been found useful for predicting job success in some kinds of work. This is tested in a variety of ways, from vocabulary lists to questions about current events. Basic background in some field of work, such as sociology or economics, may be sampled in a group of questions. Often these are principles which have become familiar to most persons through exposure rather than through formal training. It is difficult to advise you how to study for these questions; being alert to the world around you is our best suggestion.

2) Verbal ability

An example of an ability needed in many positions is verbal or language ability. Verbal ability is, in brief, the ability to use and understand words. Vocabulary and grammar tests are typical measures of this ability. Reading comprehension or paragraph interpretation questions are common in many kinds of civil service tests. You are given a paragraph of written material and asked to find its central meaning.

IV. KINDS OF QUESTIONS

1. Multiple-choice Questions

Most popular of the short-answer questions is the "multiple choice" or "best answer" question. It can be used, for example, to test for factual knowledge, ability to solve problems or judgment in meeting situations found at work.

A multiple-choice question is normally one of three types:

- It can begin with an incomplete statement followed by several possible endings. You are to find the one ending which *best* completes the statement, although some of the others may not be entirely wrong.
- It can also be a complete statement in the form of a question which is answered by choosing one of the statements listed.
- It can be in the form of a problem – again you select the best answer.

Here is an example of a multiple-choice question with a discussion which should give you some clues as to the method for choosing the right answer:

When an employee has a complaint about his assignment, the action which will *best* help him overcome his difficulty is to
A. discuss his difficulty with his coworkers
B. take the problem to the head of the organization
C. take the problem to the person who gave him the assignment
D. say nothing to anyone about his complaint

In answering this question, you should study each of the choices to find which is best. Consider choice "A" – Certainly an employee may discuss his complaint with fellow employees, but no change or improvement can result, and the complaint remains unresolved. Choice "B" is a poor choice since the head of the organization probably does not know what assignment you have been given, and taking your problem to him is known as "going over the head" of the supervisor. The supervisor, or person who made the assignment, is the person who can clarify it or correct any injustice. Choice "C" is, therefore, correct. To say nothing, as in choice "D," is unwise. Supervisors have and interest in knowing the problems employees are facing, and the employee is seeking a solution to his problem.

2. True/False

3. Matching Questions

Matching an answer from a column of choices within another column.

V. RECORDING YOUR ANSWERS

Computer terminals are used more and more today for many different kinds of exams.

For an examination with very few applicants, you may be told to record your answers in the test booklet itself. Separate answer sheets are much more common. If this separate answer sheet is to be scored by machine – and this is often the case – it is highly important that you mark your answers correctly in order to get credit.

VI. BEFORE THE TEST

YOUR PHYSICAL CONDITION IS IMPORTANT

If you are not well, you can't do your best work on tests. If you are half asleep, you can't do your best either. Here are some tips:

1) Get about the same amount of sleep you usually get. Don't stay up all night before the test, either partying or worrying—DON'T DO IT!
2) If you wear glasses, be sure to wear them when you go to take the test. This goes for hearing aids, too.
3) If you have any physical problems that may keep you from doing your best, be sure to tell the person giving the test. If you are sick or in poor health, you relay cannot do your best on any test. You can always come back and take the test some other time.

Common sense will help you find procedures to follow to get ready for an examination. Too many of us, however, overlook these sensible measures. Indeed, nervousness and fatigue have been found to be the most serious reasons why applicants fail to do their best on civil service tests. Here is a list of reminders:

- Begin your preparation early – Don't wait until the last minute to go scurrying around for books and materials or to find out what the position is all about.
- Prepare continuously – An hour a night for a week is better than an all-night cram session. This has been definitely established. What is more, a night a week for a month will return better dividends than crowding your study into a shorter period of time.
- Locate the place of the exam – You have been sent a notice telling you when and where to report for the examination. If the location is in a different town or otherwise unfamiliar to you, it would be well to inquire the best route and learn something about the building.
- Relax the night before the test – Allow your mind to rest. Do not study at all that night. Plan some mild recreation or diversion; then go to bed early and get a good night's sleep.
- Get up early enough to make a leisurely trip to the place for the test – This way unforeseen events, traffic snarls, unfamiliar buildings, etc. will not upset you.

- Dress comfortably – A written test is not a fashion show. You will be known by number and not by name, so wear something comfortable.
- Leave excess paraphernalia at home – Shopping bags and odd bundles will get in your way. You need bring only the items mentioned in the official notice you received; usually everything you need is provided. Do not bring reference books to the exam. They will only confuse those last minutes and be taken away from you when in the test room.
- Arrive somewhat ahead of time – If because of transportation schedules you must get there very early, bring a newspaper or magazine to take your mind off yourself while waiting.
- Locate the examination room – When you have found the proper room, you will be directed to the seat or part of the room where you will sit. Sometimes you are given a sheet of instructions to read while you are waiting. Do not fill out any forms until you are told to do so; just read them and be prepared.
- Relax and prepare to listen to the instructions
- If you have any physical problem that may keep you from doing your best, be sure to tell the test administrator. If you are sick or in poor health, you really cannot do your best on the exam. You can come back and take the test some other time.

VII. AT THE TEST

The day of the test is here and you have the test booklet in your hand. The temptation to get going is very strong. Caution! There is more to success than knowing the right answers. You must know how to identify your papers and understand variations in the type of short-answer question used in this particular examination. Follow these suggestions for maximum results from your efforts:

1) Cooperate with the monitor
The test administrator has a duty to create a situation in which you can be as much at ease as possible. He will give instructions, tell you when to begin, check to see that you are marking your answer sheet correctly, and so on. He is not there to guard you, although he will see that your competitors do not take unfair advantage. He wants to help you do your best.

2) Listen to all instructions
Don't jump the gun! Wait until you understand all directions. In most civil service tests you get more time than you need to answer the questions. So don't be in a hurry. Read each word of instructions until you clearly understand the meaning. Study the examples, listen to all announcements and follow directions. Ask questions if you do not understand what to do.

3) Identify your papers
Civil service exams are usually identified by number only. You will be assigned a number; you must not put your name on your test papers. Be sure to copy your number correctly. Since more than one exam may be given, copy your exact examination title.

4) Plan your time
Unless you are told that a test is a "speed" or "rate of work" test, speed itself is usually not important. Time enough to answer all the questions will be provided, but this

does not mean that you have all day. An overall time limit has been set. Divide the total time (in minutes) by the number of questions to determine the approximate time you have for each question.

5) Do not linger over difficult questions

If you come across a difficult question, mark it with a paper clip (useful to have along) and come back to it when you have been through the booklet. One caution if you do this – be sure to skip a number on your answer sheet as well. Check often to be sure that you have not lost your place and that you are marking in the row numbered the same as the question you are answering.

6) Read the questions

Be sure you know what the question asks! Many capable people are unsuccessful because they failed to *read* the questions correctly.

7) Answer all questions

Unless you have been instructed that a penalty will be deducted for incorrect answers, it is better to guess than to omit a question.

8) Speed tests

It is often better NOT to guess on speed tests. It has been found that on timed tests people are tempted to spend the last few seconds before time is called in marking answers at random – without even reading them – in the hope of picking up a few extra points. To discourage this practice, the instructions may warn you that your score will be "corrected" for guessing. That is, a penalty will be applied. The incorrect answers will be deducted from the correct ones, or some other penalty formula will be used.

9) Review your answers

If you finish before time is called, go back to the questions you guessed or omitted to give them further thought. Review other answers if you have time.

10) Return your test materials

If you are ready to leave before others have finished or time is called, take ALL your materials to the monitor and leave quietly. Never take any test material with you. The monitor can discover whose papers are not complete, and taking a test booklet may be grounds for disqualification.

VIII. EXAMINATION TECHNIQUES

1) Read the general instructions carefully. These are usually printed on the first page of the exam booklet. As a rule, these instructions refer to the timing of the examination; the fact that you should not start work until the signal and must stop work at a signal, etc. If there are any *special* instructions, such as a choice of questions to be answered, make sure that you note this instruction carefully.

2) When you are ready to start work on the examination, that is as soon as the signal has been given, read the instructions to each question booklet, underline any key words or phrases, such as *least, best, outline, describe*

and the like. In this way you will tend to answer as requested rather than discover on reviewing your paper that you *listed without describing*, that you selected the *worst* choice rather than the *best* choice, etc.

3) If the examination is of the objective or multiple-choice type – that is, each question will also give a series of possible answers: A, B, C or D, and you are called upon to select the best answer and write the letter next to that answer on your answer paper – it is advisable to start answering each question in turn. There may be anywhere from 50 to 100 such questions in the three or four hours allotted and you can see how much time would be taken if you read through all the questions before beginning to answer any. Furthermore, if you come across a question or group of questions which you know would be difficult to answer, it would undoubtedly affect your handling of all the other questions.

4) If the examination is of the essay type and contains but a few questions, it is a moot point as to whether you should read all the questions before starting to answer any one. Of course, if you are given a choice – say five out of seven and the like – then it is essential to read all the questions so you can eliminate the two that are most difficult. If, however, you are asked to answer all the questions, there may be danger in trying to answer the easiest one first because you may find that you will spend too much time on it. The best technique is to answer the first question, then proceed to the second, etc.

5) Time your answers. Before the exam begins, write down the time it started, then add the time allowed for the examination and write down the time it must be completed, then divide the time available somewhat as follows:
   - If 3-1/2 hours are allowed, that would be 210 minutes. If you have 80 objective-type questions, that would be an average of 2-1/2 minutes per question. Allow yourself no more than 2 minutes per question, or a total of 160 minutes, which will permit about 50 minutes to review.
   - If for the time allotment of 210 minutes there are 7 essay questions to answer, that would average about 30 minutes a question. Give yourself only 25 minutes per question so that you have about 35 minutes to review.

6) The most important instruction is to *read each question* and make sure you know what is wanted. The second most important instruction is to *time yourself properly* so that you answer every question. The third most important instruction is to *answer every question*. Guess if you have to but include something for each question. Remember that you will receive no credit for a blank and will probably receive some credit if you write something in answer to an essay question. If you guess a letter – say "B" for a multiple-choice question – you may have guessed right. If you leave a blank as an answer to a multiple-choice question, the examiners may respect your feelings but it will not add a point to your score. Some exams may penalize you for wrong answers, so in such cases *only*, you may not want to guess unless you have some basis for your answer.

7) Suggestions
   a. Objective-type questions
1. Examine the question booklet for proper sequence of pages and questions
2. Read all instructions carefully
3. Skip any question which seems too difficult; return to it after all other questions have been answered
4. Apportion your time properly; do not spend too much time on any single question or group of questions
5. Note and underline key words – *all, most, fewest, least, best, worst, same, opposite,* etc.
6. Pay particular attention to negatives
7. Note unusual option, e.g., unduly long, short, complex, different or similar in content to the body of the question
8. Observe the use of "hedging" words – *probably, may, most likely,* etc.
9. Make sure that your answer is put next to the same number as the question
10. Do not second-guess unless you have good reason to believe the second answer is definitely more correct
11. Cross out original answer if you decide another answer is more accurate; do not erase until you are ready to hand your paper in
12. Answer all questions; guess unless instructed otherwise
13. Leave time for review

   b. Essay questions
1. Read each question carefully
2. Determine exactly what is wanted. Underline key words or phrases.
3. Decide on outline or paragraph answer
4. Include many different points and elements unless asked to develop any one or two points or elements
5. Show impartiality by giving pros and cons unless directed to select one side only
6. Make and write down any assumptions you find necessary to answer the questions
7. Watch your English, grammar, punctuation and choice of words
8. Time your answers; don't crowd material

8) Answering the essay question

Most essay questions can be answered by framing the specific response around several key words or ideas. Here are a few such key words or ideas:

M's: manpower, materials, methods, money, management
P's: purpose, program, policy, plan, procedure, practice, problems, pitfalls, personnel, public relations
a. Six basic steps in handling problems:
1. Preliminary plan and background development
2. Collect information, data and facts
3. Analyze and interpret information, data and facts
4. Analyze and develop solutions as well as make recommendations

5. Prepare report and sell recommendations
6. Install recommendations and follow up effectiveness

b. Pitfalls to avoid
1. *Taking things for granted* – A statement of the situation does not necessarily imply that each of the elements is necessarily true; for example, a complaint may be invalid and biased so that all that can be taken for granted is that a complaint has been registered
2. *Considering only one side of a situation* – Wherever possible, indicate several alternatives and then point out the reasons you selected the best one
3. *Failing to indicate follow up* – Whenever your answer indicates action on your part, make certain that you will take proper follow-up action to see how successful your recommendations, procedures or actions turn out to be
4. *Taking too long in answering any single question* – Remember to time your answers properly

EXAMINATION SECTION

EXAMINATION SECTION

TEST 1

DIRECTIONS: Each question or incomplete statement is followed by several suggested answers or completions. Select the one that BEST answers the question or completes the statement. *PRINT THE LETTER OF THE CORRECT ANSWER IN THE SPACE AT THE RIGHT.*

1. Screening for hearing loss resulting from noise levels in the workplace is an example of _____ prevention.
   A. Primary   B. Secondary   C. Tertiary   D. Quaternary

   1.____

2. An occupational health nurse doing a walk-through to identify workplace hazards is providing _____ prevention.
   A. Primary   B. Secondary   C. Tertiary   D. Quaternary

   2.____

3. Limited duty programs after a cumulative trauma injury is an example of _____ prevention.
   A. Primary   B. Secondary   C. Tertiary   D. Quaternary

   3.____

4. If an occupational health nurse refers an employee to an employee assistance program, what problem will MOST likely be addressed?
   A. Obesity   B. Hypertension
   C. Alcohol abuse   D. Smoking cessation

   4.____

5. When working as an occupational health nurse, which of the following is the BEST primary prevention tactic?
   A. Performing a worksite walk-through
   B. Providing education for personal protective equipment
   C. Obtaining accurate and thorough employee health assessments
   D. Providing screening for hearing loss and respiratory function

   5.____

6. An occupational health nurse recognized a range of practice issues and functions comfortably in the roles as clinician, coordinator, and case manager, following company procedures, utilizing assessment checklists, and clinical protocols to provide treatment
   According to AAOHN competency levels, this nurse is functioning at _____ level.
   A. Beginner   B. Competent   C. Proficient   D. Expert

   6.____

7. An occupational health nurse provides leadership in developing occupational safety and health policy within the organization, functions in upper executive or management roles, serves as a consultant to business and government, and designs and conducts significant research.
   According to AAOHN competency levels, this nurse is functioning at _____ level.
   A. Beginner   B. Competent   C. Proficient   D. Expert

   7.____

8. If an occupational health nurse quickly obtains information needed for accurate assessment and moves quickly to the critical aspects of a problem within priority setting and structural goals in response to a client situation, the nurse usually possesses sophisticated clinical or managerial skills in the work environment.
According to AAOHN competency levels, this nurse is functioning at _____ level.
   A. Beginner   B. Competent   C. Proficient   D. Expert

8.____

9. The specialty of occupational health focuses on the identification and control of risks to health that occur as a result of physical, chemical, and other workplace hazards.
Which of the following is an example of a physical hazard?
   A. Infectious agents   B. Sexual harassment
   C. Hazardous chemical exposures   D. Electric and magnetic fields

9.____

10. There are several scientific disciplines that guide the occupational health nurse in understanding the agent, host, and environment relationship.
Which of the following is one of these disciplines?
   A. Biology   B. Psychology   C. Microbiology D. Epidemiology

10.____

11. What type of injury has the HIGHEST incidence rate resulting in days away from work?
   A. Sprains   B. Fractures   C. Concussions   D. Dislocations

11.____

12. What industry has the HIGHEST number of fatal injuries occurring at the worksite?
   A. Mining   B. Agriculture   C. Healthcare   D. Construction

12.____

13. Which of the following is a characteristic of a health promotion program?
   A. Narrow focus
   B. Multidimensional
   C. Balance work and physical concerns
   D. Supports the business objectives of the organization

13.____

14. An occupational health nurse's physical assessment of a worker identifies an acute-onset pruritic dermatitis extending over the face, hands, neck, and forearms.
What should be the nurse's priority?
   A. Contact senior management, educate workers about potential exposure, and clean the area.
   B. Contact OSHA immediately and remove the chemical from the work environment.
   C. Immediately evacuate the workers in the nearby workspace and treat the worker and other exposed workers.
   D. Treat the client and obtain a comprehensive exposure history. If an on-site environment exposure is suspected as the cause, screen other at-risk workers and eliminate the environmental risk.

14.____

15. An occupational health nurse is concerned about the accuracy of the tuberculin skin test in screening individuals with tuberculosis exposure for follow-up chest radiography.
    What aspect of the test's validity is this nurse questioning?
    A. Reliability   B. Sensitivity   C. Specificity   D. Variability

15.____

16. What is the overall goal of occupational health nursing?
    A. Treat and care for injured employees
    B. Establish and maintain a safe and healthy environment for workers
    C. Develop workplace policies to ensure the health of workers
    D. Report potential workplace hazards to senior management

16.____

17. _____ is the applied science of equipment design, intended to maximize productivity by reducing operator fatigue and discomfort.
    A. Biometrics   B. Ergonomics
    C. Biomechanics   D. Kinesiology

17.____

18. What is the PRIMARY responsibility of the occupational health nurse as a clinician?
    A. Participation in the development, management, and evaluation of the entire health and safety program of the organization
    B. Investigate all possible material and chemical exposures that could lead to an adverse reaction in workers
    C. Coordination and management of services for ill or injured workers, including aspects related to group health, workers compensation, and regulations dealing with the Family Medical Leave Act
    D. To prevent work and non-work related health problems and to restore and maintain the health of workers

18.____

19. Occupational health nurses that function as _____ achieve their goals through assessments of hazards, surveillance of the workers/workplace, investigation of illness, and monitoring events that lead to an injury.
    A. Advisor   B. Clinician
    C. Coordinator   D. Care Manager

19.____

20. Which of the following is the responsibility of the occupational health nurse as a case manager?
    A. Participation in the development, management, and evaluation of the entire health and safety program of the organization
    B. Investigate all possible material and chemical exposures that could lead to an adverse reaction in workers
    C. Coordination and management of services for ill or injured workers, including aspects related to group health, workers compensation, and regulations dealing with the Family Medical Leave Act
    D. To prevent work and non-work related health problems and to restore and maintain the health of workers

20.____

21. What is the PRIMARY concern of occupational health nurses who function as case managers?   21._____
    A. Prevention and healthcare after an incident has occurred
    B. Establish and maintain a safe and healthy environment for workers
    C. Develop workplace policies to ensure the health of workers
    D. Report potential workplace health hazards to senior management

22. What is the overall goal of an occupational health nurse as a care manager?   22._____
    A. Prevention and healthcare after an incident has occurred
    B. Establish and maintain a safe and healthy environment for workers
    C. Develop workplace policies to ensure the health of workers
    D. To do everything that can be done to prevent accidents and minimize illness

23. Which of the following is a process for understanding and solving a problem, with the goal of determining what happened, why it happened, and what can be done to prevent its reoccurrence?   23.____
    A. Root cause analysis   B. Worker assessment
    C. Workplace walk-through   D. Worksite surveillance

24. A complete survey of the workplace, inside and outside, compiling information as to the presence of hazards, the location of entries and exits, the availability of emergency equipment and potential trouble spots is referred to as a   24.____
    A. root cause analysis   B. worker assessment
    C. workplace walk-through   D. worksite surveillance

25. The goal of which of the following is to identify the agent, hose, and environmental characteristics that place the worker at risk and to prevent, eliminate, or reduce adverse exposure?   25.____
    A. Root cause analysis   B. Worker assessment
    C. Workplace walk-through   D. Worksite surveillance

KEY (CORRECT ANSWERS)

1.	B		11.	A
2.	A		12.	D
3.	C		13.	B
4.	C		14.	D
5.	A		15.	B
6.	B		16.	B
7.	D		17.	B
8.	C		18.	D
9.	D		19.	B
10.	D		20.	D

21.	A
22.	D
23.	A
24.	C
25.	B

TEST 2

DIRECTIONS: Each question or incomplete statement is followed by several suggested answers or completions. Select the one that BEST answers the question or completes the statement. *PRINT THE LETTER OF THE CORRECT ANSWER IN THE SPACE AT THE RIGHT.*

1. Educating all employees and administrative staff regarding the exposures and hazards associated in the workplace is the foundation of _____ efforts?
   A. Health literacy
   B. Health prevention
   C. Health promotion
   D. Health surveillance

   1._____

2. Which of the following, which occurs in both physical and mental health, refers to employees working even though they are ill?
   A. Absenteeism
   B. Presenteeism
   C. Burnout
   D. Organizational injustice

   2._____

3. A nurse working in an occupational health setting will MOST likely function in a(n) _____ role?
   A. advisor
   B. clinician
   C. coordinator
   D. care manager

   3._____

4. Which work-related hazard may be encountered by everyone in the workforce?
   A. Hearing loss
   B. Arthritis
   C. Sprains and strains
   D. Workplace stress

   4._____

5. Which of the following represents the PRIMARY role of an occupational health nurse?
   A. Performing workplace walk-throughs
   B. Maintaining company compliance with regulatory agencies
   C. Providing health promotion and emergency care
   D. Providing health care to employees and their families

   5._____

6. Which of the following was the FIRST piece of legislation that specifically required prevention programs for workers?
   A. Mine Safety and Health Act
   B. Occupational Safety and Health Act
   C. Patient Protection and Affordable Care Act
   D. Workers' Compensation Bill of Rights

   6._____

7. What tool does the occupational health nurse rely on to understanding the complex relationships among the workers, hazards in the workplace, and hazards in the environment?
   A. Epidemiologic triad
   B. Health belief model
   C. Workers' Compensation Bill of Rights
   D. The Beveridge model

   7._____

8. Which of the following would be considered to be an "agent" in the epidemiologic triad?
   A. Family members of workers
   B. Domineering management
   C. Temperature extremes
   D. Workers with low immunity to disease

8.____

9. Which of the following would be considered to be a "host" in the epidemiologic triad?
   A. Family members of workers   B. Temperature extremes
   C. Chemical exposure   D. Overcrowded work environment

9.____

10. What population of workers are at the GREATEST risk of experiencing work-related accidents that result in injuries?
    A. Elderly employees
    B. Workers with chronic illness
    C. Women of childbearing age
    D. Workers with less than one year of experience

10.____

11. After conducting a walk-through assessment, the occupational health nurse should understand that it is easiest to decrease exposure to what hazard?
    A. Noise   B. Chemicals   C. Bacteria   D. Aerosols

11.____

12. It should be well known to the occupational health nurse that a slippery floor is an example of what type of hazard?
    A. Physical   B. Chemical
    C. Biological   D. Enviromechanical

12.____

13. For what reason would an occupational health nurse conduct an occupational health assessment?
    A. To educate works about potential hazards
    B. To determine the extent of a worker's injury
    C. To determine the etiology of a worker's disease
    D. To identify agent and host factors that place workers at risk

13.____

14. What is the overall goal of the Occupational Safety and Health Administration?
    A. To educate employers about occupational health and safety
    B. To educate occupational health and safety employees
    C. To identify and research occupational health and safety hazards
    D. To educate workplace healthcare providers on the proper way to handle injuries to workers

14.____

15. What is the overall goal of the National Institute for Occupational Safety and Health?
    A. To perform ongoing surveillance of deaths that occur in the workplace
    B. To educate employees about environmental risks and hazards
    C. To examine potential hazards of new work technologies and practices
    D. To set and maintain standards that monitor worker's exposure to toxic substances

15.____

16. Which of the commonly found workplace items would require a Material Safety Data Sheet (MSDS)?
    A. Floor scrubber
    B. Eye goggles
    C. Printer ink
    D. Lead aprons

    16.____

17. Sharing written disaster plans with key resources in the community is a requirement of what piece of legislation?
    A. Mine and Safety and Health Act
    B. Occupational Safety and Health Act
    C. Patient Protection and Affordable Care Act
    D. Superfund Amendment and Reauthorization Act

    17.____

18. What action would be the responsibility of the occupational health nurse during disaster planning?
    A. Assessing for possible disasters
    B. Preventing death and injuries of workers
    C. Ensuring MSDS sheets are in a safe but readily accessible area
    D. Collaborating with governmental and regulatory agencies to plan disaster management

    18.____

19. An occupational health nurse working in an occupational health and safety program is likely to provide all of the following services EXCEPT
    A. health screening
    B. case management
    C. health/medical surveillance
    D. referrals to medical specialists

    19.____

20. An occupational health nurse would become a member of the American Association of Occupational Health Nurses for all of the following reasons EXCEPT to
    A. promote the health and safety of workers
    B. lobby Congress for safer workplaces and work practices
    C. advance the Occupational Health Nursing profession by supporting research
    D. promote and provide continuing education in the specialty of Occupational Health Nursing

    20.____

21. If a worker is experiencing health reaction to a safe low-level exposure, he/she is experiencing
    A. anaphylaxis
    B. hypersusceptibility
    C. shigellosis
    D. metabolic syndrome

    21.____

22. Which of the following statements is TRUE regarding chemical agent?
    A. Chemicals are not ordinarily found in the body tissues of the general population.
    B. Most chemicals have been thoroughly examined to identify their health effects on humans.
    C. Chronic exposure to below standard, low-level doses of workplace chemicals constitutes a potential health risk.
    D. Human effects of chemical exposure are primarily associated with a single agent rather than with the interaction of agents.

    22.____

23. Which of the following is a systems approach that can be used by
occupational health nurses to help them organize a prevention model?
    A. Epidemiologic triad   B. Health belief model
    C. Balance theory   D. The Beveridge model

23.____

24. If it is the duty of the occupational health nurse to investigate the nature of
the workplace incident, the part of the body involved, the source of the illness
or injury, the circumstances that resulted in the event, and then perform a root
cause analysis, this nurse is functioning in what role?
    A. Advisor   B. Clinician
    C. Coordinator   D. Care Manager

24.____

25. Investigating all possible material and chemical exposures that could lead
to an adverse reaction in workers because, by law, workers and their
advocates have a right to know the substances to which they may be exposed
and therefore may request requisite information is the responsibility of what
role of an occupational health nurse?
    A. Advisor   B. Clinician
    C. Coordinator   D. Care Manager

25.____

KEY (CORRECT ANSWERS)

1.	C		11.	A
2.	B		12.	D
3.	B		13.	D
4.	D		14.	A
5.	C		15.	C
6.	A		16.	C
7.	A		17.	D
8.	C		18.	D
9.	A		19.	D
10.	D		20.	D

21.	B
22.	C
23.	C
24.	D
25.	A

TEST 3

DIRECTIONS: Each question or incomplete statement is followed by several suggested answers or completions. Select the one that BEST answers the question or completes the statement. *PRINT THE LETTER OF THE CORRECT ANSWER IN THE SPACE AT THE RIGHT.*

1. If the duties of an occupational health nurse include participating in the development, management, and evaluation of the entire health and safety program of the organization, in conjunction with both the medical and safety directors, in what role is this nurse practicing?
   A. Advisor
   B. Clinician
   C. Coordinator
   D. Care Manager

1.____

2. If a care manager is required to perform a root cause analysis, what would be the initial step?
   A. Collect data
   B. Define the problem
   C. Identify the root cause
   D. Identify possible causal factors

2.____

3. If an occupational health nurse creates an environment for the worker that provides a sense of balance among work, family, personal, health, and psychosocial concerns, which of the following does this represent?
   A. Health literacy
   B. Health prevention
   C. Health promotion
   D. Health surveillance

3.____

4. Which of the following is defined as clusters of the same diagnosis collected from a specific population within a distinct period of time?
   A. Mortality
   B. Morbidity
   C. Incidence
   D. Prevalence

4.____

5. The total burden of injury or illness that exists in the population is referred to as
   A. mortality
   B. morbidity
   C. incidence
   D. prevalence

5.____

6. What organization requires the occupational health nurse to keep a log that is used to report total injuries and illnesses annually?
   A. U.S. Department of Labor
   B. National Occupational Research Agenda
   C. Occupational Safety and Health Administration
   D. National Institute of Occupational Safety and Health

6.____

7. Which of the following is a partnership program that functions to stimulate innovative methods and improved practices for safer, healthier workplaces?
   A. U.S. Department of Labor
   B. National Occupational Research Agenda
   C. Occupational Safety and Health Administration
   D. National Institute of Occupational Safety and Health

7.____

8. What type of epidemiologic study is used to investigate workers who have been exposed to a variety of chemical, biological, or physical agents?
   A. Cohort studies
   B. Ecologic studies
   C. Case-control studies
   D. Cross-sectional studies

8.____

9. What type of epidemiologic study is used to investigate what agent or set of agents are responsible for causing a particular medical condition?
   A. Cohort studies
   B. Ecologic studies
   C. Case-control studies
   D. Cross-sectional studies

9.____

10. What type of epidemiologic studies are used to compare the rates of exposures and diseases in different populations?
    A. Cohort studies
    B. Ecologic studies
    C. Case-control studies
    D. Cross-sectional studies

10.____

11. What type of hazard poses the GREATEST threat to healthcare workers?
    A. Physical
    B. Chemical
    C. Biological
    D. Enviromechanical

11.____

12. What is the MOST common route of occupational exposure to chemicals?
    A. Skin contact
    B. Ingestion
    C. Inhalation
    D. Through open cuts/abrasions

12.____

13. Which of the following statements BEST describes the chemical exposure term "permissible exposure limit"?
    A. An exposure with no adverse effects anticipated
    B. Any workplace exposure that can never be exceeded
    C. Maximum exposure allowed by OSHA during an 8-hour period
    D. A workplace exposure which, if exceeded, will result in harmful medical conditions

13.____

14. What organization is responsible for regulating the disposal of biologically infectious wastes from workplaces?
    A. Occupational Safety and Health Organization
    B. Environmental Protection Agency
    C. Centers for Disease Control and Prevention
    D. Agency for Toxic Substances and Disease Registry

14.____

15. What organization, other than The Joint Commission, has been granted deemed status to provide accreditation to healthcare facilities?
    A. The American Medical Association
    B. The American Osteopathic Association
    C. The Occupational Safety and Health Administration
    D. The National Institute for Occupational Safety and Health

15.____

16. What term is used when an employee's work measurably heightens their chances of being harmed in comparison to the general public?
    A. Actual risk
    B. Peculiar risk
    C. Positional risk
    D. Increased risk

16.____

17. What term is generally used when harm would not have occurred but for the fact that the employee's job placed them in a situation in which they were harmed?
    A. Actual risk
    B. Peculiar risk
    C. Positional risk
    D. Increased risk

17.____

18. Environment and exposure are two of the five issues that need to be considered when performing a hazard analysis.
All of the following are issues that should also be included EXCEPT
    A. trigger
    B. compliance
    C. consequence
    D. feeder factors

18.____

19. What term describes a chemical exposure level that should never be exceeded?
    A. Ceiling limit
    B. Threshold limit
    C. Recommended exposure limit
    D. Minimum occupational exposure limit

19.____

20. All of the following are included in the seven (7) joint commission environment of care management plans EXCEPT
    A. fire safety
    B. infection control
    C. hazardous materials
    D. medical equipment management

20.____

21. What is the MOST important objective of a workplace safety program?
    A. Prevent possible litigation actions
    B. Avoid regulatory citations and fines
    C. Increase organizational effectiveness and reduce costs
    D. To promote employee relations and reduction of employee turnover

21.____

22. Which of the following is a well-known process used to break down jobs or tasks for the purpose of identifying hazards and implementing controls to prevent potential injuries?
    A. Total quality management
    B. Job time and motion study
    C. Tasks continuous quality improvement
    D. Job safety or job hazard analysis

22.____

23. What action would be MOST effective to reduce infection rates among workers in any organization?
    A. Ensure the environment is cleaned thoroughly after every shift
    B. Encourage the use of workers wearing personal protective equipment
    C. Require frequent handwashing or sanitizing by all workers at the facility
    D. Implement proper CDC isolation controls for workers who are ill or contagious

23.____

24. What is the OSHA exposure limit that requires a hearing conservation program to be in place?
    A. 65 dB   B. 75 dB   C. 85 dB   D. 95 dB

24.____

25. Which of the following occurs when the combined effects of several different exposures is greater than the sum of the individual exposures?

    A. Latency
    B. Synergism
    C. Anaphylaxis
    D. Hyper susceptibility

25._____

KEY (CORRECT ANSWERS)

1.	C		11.	C
2.	B		12.	C
3.	C		13.	C
4.	C		14.	D
5.	C		15.	B
6.	C		16.	D
7.	C		17.	D
8.	A		18.	B
9.	C		19.	C
10.	B		20.	B

21.	C
22.	D
23.	C
24.	C
25.	B

TEST 4

DIRECTIONS: Each question or incomplete statement is followed by several suggested answers or completions. Select the one that BEST answers the question or completes the statement. *PRINT THE LETTER OF THE CORRECT ANSWER IN THE SPACE AT THE RIGHT.*

1. All of the following are components of an occupational health history EXCEPT
    A. characteristics of the worker's previous jobs
    B. chronological record of all past work and potential exposures
    C. an occupational exposure inventory
    D. list of other exposures in the home or community

1.____

2. Which of the following statements is TRUE regarding exposure to occupational hazards?
Exposure
    A. varies with individual susceptibility to the harmful effects of the hazardous agents
    B. is most reliably measured by placing personal sampling devices on the worker while at work
    C. at levels below the legal occupational exposure limit cannot result in adverse health effects
    D. will result in irreversible effects on health if the legal occupational exposure limit is exceeded

2.____

3. If the license of an occupational health nurse requires continuing education, courses focusing on what topics would be MOST useful?
    A. Diversity and bioethics
    B. Ergonomics and toxicology
    C. Evaluating risks and personnel management
    D. Health assessment and home health care

3.____

4. For what reason did the role of occupational health nurse undergo such rapid expansion throughout the 20th century?
    A. Cost savings were able to be documented to employers.
    B. Nurses were able to promote the role and its benefits to the media.
    C. Legislation required employers to provide certain amenities and nurses were most qualified to provide these.
    D. Legislation required an occupational health nurse at any site with more than fifty employees.

4.____

5. Which of the following is the MOST challenging aspect of the role of occupational health nurse?
    A. Allocating time for both direct service to employees and management tasks
    B. Collaborating with other work site professionals and retaining leadership in the arena of employee health
    C. Ethical conflicts between responsibilities to management and responsibilities to employees
    D. Maintaining competence through attending conferences and maintaining services when the nurse is absent

    5.____

6. What is the danger/hazard that is brought forth by an etiological agent?
    A. Asphyxiation
    B. Human disease
    C. Corrosive reaction
    D. Allergic reaction

    6.____

7. If an employee moves employees who have reached upper permissible level of exposure to a hazardous environment to prevent further exposure is what type of hazard control?
    A. Personal control
    B. Professional control
    C. Administrative control
    D. Engineering control

    7.____

8. Quantitative risk assessment usually measures human exposure through all of the following methods EXCEPT
    A. personal surveys
    B. computer models
    C. toxicological analysis
    D. blood or urine analysis

    8.____

9. What document required by the Occupational Safety and Health Administration (OSHA) is to contain a plan for post-exposure evaluation and follow-up?
    A. Exposure control plan
    B. Employee medical records
    C. Occupational risk assessment
    D. Employee health assessment

    9.____

10. Which of the following training is required by the Hazard Communication Standard from the Occupational Safety and Health Administration (OSHA)?
    A. An explanation of the exposure control plan
    B. The value of receiving the hepatitis B vaccine
    C. Physical and health hazards of chemicals in the work area
    D. Information on the epidemiology of specific infectious disease

    10.____

11. Which of the following would represent an engineering control?
    A. Using a device to isolate or remove a hazard
    B. Altering the manner in which a task is performed
    C. Hiring a licensed engineer to review the mechanical aspects of the building
    D. Maintaining building air conditioning and heating systems in good working order

    11.____

12. A(n) _____ diagram is a tool that enables the occupational health nurse to identify, explore, and graphically display the possible causes of an incident or hazardous condition.

    A. matrix   B. affinity
    C. fishbone   D. inter-relationship

12._____

13. What did the Occupational Safety and Health Act of 1970 require?

    A. A free health examination to all employees prior to beginning employment
    B. Employers are required to make suggestions on standards for improving worker safety
    C. Employers have the right to request an OSHA inspection for a way to improve work site safety
    D. Employers must keep the work site free from recognized hazards

13._____

14. Which of the following would be an example of what the Code of Federal Regulations Title 29 requires of the occupational health nurse?

    A. All employees must be trained in first aid and CPR.
    B. Work-related injuries, illnesses, and death records must be posted yearly.
    C. The occupational health nurse must serve as an emergency warden, helping employees to the emergency exit in safe manner.
    D. The occupational health nurse must accompany OSHA inspectors during the yearly work site inspection.

14._____

15. What responsibility does the occupational health nurse have in relation to an injured employee and the Workers' Compensation Act?

    A. To assist the employee in obtaining legal representation to negotiate a financial settlement
    B. To assist the employer to work out a settlement with the employee to avoid legal suits against the employer
    C. To file a claim for the employee with Workers' Compensation to ensure continued full salary until the employee is able to return to work
    D. To work with the employee to keep the employee informed, limit disability, and provide opportunity for rapid return to employment

15._____

16. All of the following are required after a work-related injury or illness occurs EXCEPT

    A. initial assessment
    B. documentation of the incident
    C. medical record initiation
    D. complete medical and family history

16._____

17. From an occupational health standpoint, which of the following is defined as an abnormal condition or disorder that is caused by exposure to environmental factors?

    A. Injury   B. Illness   C. Trauma   D. Disability

17._____

18. From an occupational health perspective, carpal tunnel would be classified as what type of medical condition?
    A. Injury
    B. Disability
    C. Acute trauma
    D. Cumulative trauma

18.____

19. Incompatibility between workplace design and human physiology is the cause of what type of hazards?
    A. Physical
    B. Chemical
    C. Biological
    D. Enviromechanical

19.____

20. The Employee Assistance Program is a federal system designed to alleviate the effects of what type of workplace hazard?
    A. Physical
    B. Biological
    C. Psychosocial
    D. Enviromechanical

20.____

21. If an employee suffers from a serious health condition, what piece of legislation allows them to take 12 weeks of unpaid, job-protected leave in a 12-month period?
    A. Family Medical Leave Act
    B. Occupational Safety and Health Act
    C. Patient Protection and Affordable Care Act
    D. Americans with Disabilities Act

21.____

22. From an occupational health perspective, which of the following is defined as a physical or mental impairment that substantially limits one or more major life activities?
    A. Injury   B. Illness   C. Trauma   D. Disability

22.____

23. Which of the following is a form of hazard control that relies on management actions such as worker training, work scheduling to reduce exposure times, and development and use of safe work practices?
    A. Environmental controls
    B. Professional controls
    C. Administrative controls
    D. Engineering controls

23.____

24. Which of the following is a method of hazard control designed to address the hazard at the source?
    A. Environmental controls
    B. Professional controls
    C. Administrative controls
    D. Engineering controls

24.____

25. _____ requires the continual evaluation of the workplace and employees for potential exposure which involves worksite inspections and surveys, environmental monitoring, evaluation of the results, and interpretation of the findings.
    A. Exposure monitoring
    B. Worker assessment
    C. Workplace walk-through
    D. Worksite surveillance

25.____

KEY (CORRECT ANSWERS)

1.	A
2.	A
3.	B
4.	A
5.	B
6.	B
7.	C
8.	B
9.	A
10.	C

11.	D
12.	C
13.	D
14.	B
15.	D
16.	D
17.	B
18.	D
19.	D
20.	C

21.	A
22.	D
23.	C
24.	D
25.	A

EXAMINATION SECTION

TEST 1

DIRECTIONS: Each question or incomplete statement is followed by several suggested answers or completions. Select the one that BEST answers the question or completes the statement. *PRINT THE LETTER OF THE CORRECT ANSWER IN THE SPACE AT THE RIGHT.*

1. Chemical exposure to which of the following chemicals is associated with a liver cancer called angiosarcoma?
   A. Lead
   B. Asbestos
   C. Vinyl chloride
   D. Trichloroethylene
   1.____

2. Olfactory fatigue is a phenomenon associated with which of the following substances?
   A. Phosgene
   B. Diethylamine
   C. Sulfuric acid
   D. Hydrogen sulfide
   2.____

3. What chemical has the sweet smell of fresh mowed grass but is highly toxic?
   A. Phosgene
   B. Diethylamine
   C. Sulfuric acid
   D. Hydrogen sulfide
   3.____

4. What chemical has the terrible smell of rotten fish but is only mildly toxic?
   A. Phosgene
   B. Diethylamine
   C. Sulfuric acid
   D. Hydrogen sulfide
   4.____

5. What type of chemicals commonly extract the natural oils and fats from the skin, causing the skin to become dry and irritated?
   A. Acids
   B. Bases
   C. Ethers
   D. Organic solvents
   5.____

6. A chemical which, because of its specific toxic effect on biochemical mechanisms in the body prevents the body from absorbing, transporting, or utilizing oxygen for the production of usable energy is referred to as a _____ asphyxiant.
   A. simple
   B. general
   C. complex
   D. chemical
   6.____

7. Which of the following is an organic solvent that affects the nervous system and can cause peripheral neuropathy?
   A. n-hexane
   B. Vinyl chloride
   C. Hydrogen sulfide
   D. Carbon tetrachloride
   7.____

8. Organic solvents are generally fat-soluble; therefore, they are referred to as being
   A. lipophilic
   B. lipophobic
   C. hydrophilic
   D. hydrophobic
   8.____

9. Which of the following workplace chemicals can specifically cause damage to the kidneys?

    A. Silica   B. Propanol   C. Lead salts   D. Vinyl chloride

9.____

10. Poisoning due to what chemical can cause the red blood cells to swell, break open, and release inorganic arsenic into the bloodstream?

    A. Arsine   B. Ammonia
    C. Methanol   D. Carbon monoxide

10.____

11. Which chemical damages the blood forming cells of the bone marrow?

    A. Benzene   B. Ammonia
    C. Methanol   D. Carbon monoxide

11.____

12. Which of the following is the MOST common type of asbestos found in the North American workplace?

    A. Silicate   B. Crysotile   C. Fiberglass   D. Isocyanate

12.____

13. Which chemical family has the capacity to sensitize the lungs and cause severe asthmatic reactions in some people at very low levels?

    A. Ethers   B. Peroxides
    C. Isocyanates   D. Benzene compounds

13.____

14. What type of acid can penetrate the tissues and deplete the body of calcium and will cause death without early and specialized treatment?

    A. Acetic   B. Muriatic   C. Phosphoric   D. Hydrofluoric

14.____

15. Holes in the nasal septum can be the result of exposure to what chemical?

    A. Arsenic   B. Creosol   C. Turpentine   D. Formaldehyde

16.____

16. Metals and metal salts can have all of the following effects on the skin EXCEPT

    A. skin cancer   B. dry and de-fatted skin
    C. irritation and ulceration   D. spotty-colored areas of the skin

17.____

17. Which of the following is the main effect of oxidizing agents, such as hydrogen peroxide, on the skin?

    A. Skin cancer   B. Dermatitis
    C. Skin discoloration   D. Alopecia

18.____

18. _____ sampling is a type of sampling method used to identify peak or ceiling concentrations of contaminant during a time of high production.

    A. Area   B. Grab   C. Personal   D. Integrated

19.____

19. _____ sampling is a type of air sampling typically used to estimate a worker's 8 hour time-weighted average (TWA) exposure or 15-minute short-term exposure limit (STEL).

    A. Area   B. Grab   C. Personal   D. Integrated

20.____

20. What part of the ear is responsible for maintaining balance?
    A. Pinna   B. Cochlea
    C. Ossicles   D. Semicircular canals

21. What area of the cochlea contains sensitive hair cells which can cause hearing loss if damaged?
    A. Spiral ganglion   B. Organ of Corti
    C. Scala tympani   D. Tectorial membrane

22. One of the bones of the middle ear is called the incus, which is commonly referred to as the
    A. anvil   B. stirrup   C. mallet   D. hammer

23. Which of the following refers to the units used to measure sound pressure?
    A. Ohms   B. Pascals   C. Decibels   D. Sieverts

24. When the sound intensity from a source is doubled, the approximate decibel level increased by how much?
    A. 3   B. 4   C. 5   D. 6

25. A _____ is a very fine solid aerosol particle formed when a vaporized solid condenses in air.
    A. gas   B. fume   C. mist   D. vapor

21._____

21._____

22._____

23._____

24._____

25._____

KEY (CORRECT ANSWERS)

1.	C	11.	A
2.	C	12.	D
3.	A	13.	C
4.	B	14.	D
5.	D	15.	A
6.	C	16.	B
7.	A	17.	B
8.	A	18.	B
9.	C	19.	D
10.	A	20.	D

21.	B
22.	A
23.	B
24.	A
25.	B

TEST 2

DIRECTIONS: Each question or incomplete statement is followed by several suggested answers or completions. Select the one that BEST answers the question or completes the statement. *PRINT THE LETTER OF THE CORRECT ANSWER IN THE SPACE AT THE RIGHT.*

1. Through what method does cyanide act as a chemical asphyxiant?
   A. By inhibiting enzymes in the mitochondria of cells
   B. By killing the cells in the alveoli walls which inhibits gas exchange
   C. By narrowing the bronchioles so that air cannot get to the alveoli
   D. By combining with hemoglobin to reduce the blood's ability to carry oxygen to the cells

   1.____

2. Which of the following statements are TRUE regarding chemical exposures?
   A. Non-polar chemicals dissolve readily in water.
   B. Positive and negative charges on organic chemicals are removed by liver enzymes.
   C. The liver turns non-polar chemicals into polar chemicals so they can be excreted by the kidneys.
   D. The liver converts organic solvents to fats so they can be eliminated by the body in the urine.

   2.____

3. Local effects of chemicals on the skin are relatively easy to prevent through which of the following methods?
   A. Local ventilation
   B. The use of gloves
   C. Screening workers for skin sensitivities upon hire
   D. Having an antidote readily available

   3.____

4. All of the following effects on the skin can be typically caused by insecticides EXCEPT
   A. chloracne   B. dermatitis   C. melanoma   D. spotty skin

   4.____

5. What material is BEST for shielding gamma radiation?
   A. Lead   B. Wood   C. Aluminum   D. Tungsten

   5.____

6. Which of the following statements is TRUE regarding the stochastic effects of ionizing radiation?
   A. They occur immediately following radiation exposure.
   B. They are clearly observable.
   C. They only occur after exposure to large doses.
   D. They tend to result in cancers or genetic damage.

   6.____

7. Which of the following statements is TRUE regarding the deterministic effects of ionizing radiation?
   A. They only occur after exposure to low doses.
   B. They only occur after exposure to high doses.
   C. They tend to result in cancers or genetic damage.
   D. They are clearly observable such as skin reddening.

   7.____

8. What type of radiation detector is a direct-reading, portable unit that allows a worker to see their radiation dose while working with a radiation source?
   A. Film badge
   B. Pocket dosimeter
   C. Ionization chamber
   D. Thermal luminescence dosimeter

8.____

9. Which of the following represents the MINIMUM amount of shielding required to stop alpha radiation?
   A. A piece of paper
   B. A ½ inch of aluminum
   C. 1 inch of wood
   D. Several inches of lead

9.____

10. Which of the following represents the MINIMUM amount of shielding required to stop beta radiation?
   A. A piece of paper
   B. A ½ inch of aluminum
   C. 1 inch of wood
   D. Several inches of lead

10.____

11. _____ are the volatile form of substances that are normally in the solid or liquid state at room temperature and pressure.
   A. Mists
   B. Gases
   C. Fumes
   D. Vapors

11.____

12. _____ is a general term that refers to the response of the lungs to inhaled dust.
   A. Pneumonitis
   B. Pneumonia
   C. Pneumoconiosis
   D. Pneumothorax

12.____

13. Which of the following refers to a chemical that is foreign to the body, not produced by the body, and is therefore not expected to be there?
   A. Probiotic
   B. Antibiotic
   C. Xenobiotic
   D. Macrobiotic

13.____

14. What type of effects occur when a substance that normally has no toxic effect becomes toxic in the presence of another substance? For example, trichloroethylene interferes with the liver in the presence of carbon tetrachloride.
   A. Additive
   B. Synergistic
   C. Antagonistic
   D. Potentiating

14.____

15. Which of the following processes, also known as biotransformation, is the transformation of chemicals in the body which makes them more water soluble for excretion?
   A. Metabolism
   B. Sequestration
   C. Oxidation
   D. Mastication

15.____

16. Which of the following refers to a substance that causes birth defects in a developing fetus?
   A. Toxicant
   B. Pathogen
   C. Carcinogen
   D. Teratogen

16.____

17. The Ames Test is used to determine what characteristic of a substance?
   A. Pathogenicity
   B. Teratogenicity
   C. Mutagenicity
   D. Carcinogenicity

17.____

18. Urticarial reactions occur in what organ of the body?   18._____
    A. Eyes   B. Skin   C. Liver   D. Heart

19. Which of the following chemicals could potentially be a teratogen?   19._____
    A. Silica   B. Asbestos
    C. Carbon dioxide   D. Organic mercury

20. Nicotine is BEST described by what toxic property?   20._____
    A. Hepatotoxin   B. Neurotoxin   C. Teratogen   D. Carcinogen

21. Organochlorines have the ability to cause adverse effects to the _____   21._____
    system of the human body.
    A. integumentary   B. central nervous
    C. musculoskeletal   D. cardiovascular

22. Exposure to what element is associated with Parkinson-like symptoms?   22._____
    A. Lead   B. Mercury   C. Manganese   D. Magnesium

23. Heavy metals are stored in what location of the human body?   23._____
    A. Fats   B. Liver   C. Bones   D. Spleen

24. The common cold, polio, rabies, and hepatitis are all examples of   24._____
    A. viruses   B. fungi   C. bacteria   D. protozoa

25. What is the latency period for asbestos-related diseases?   25._____
    A. 1 year   B. 3 years   C. 10 years   D. 30 years

————

KEY (CORRECT ANSWERS)

1.	A		11.	D
2.	C		12.	C
3.	B		13.	C
4.	C		14.	D
5.	A		15.	A
6.	D		16.	D
7.	D		17.	C
8.	B		18.	B
9.	A		19.	D
10.	B		20.	B

21.	B
22.	C
23.	C
24.	A
25.	D

TEST 3

DIRECTIONS: Each question or incomplete statement is followed by several suggested answers or completions. Select the one that BEST answers the question or completes the statement. *PRINT THE LETTER OF THE CORRECT ANSWER IN THE SPACE AT THE RIGHT.*

1. What type of asbestos fibers has been banned for use in the United States?
   A. Amosite   B. Tremolite   C. Chyrsotile   D. Crocidolite

   1.____

2. What is the core body temperature that would be indicative of heat stress for acclimated personnel?
   A. 9.5°F   B. 100.3°F   C. 100.8°F   D. 101.3°F

   2.____

3. What environmental factor has a synergistic effect on Raynaud's Syndrome?
   A. Heat   B. Cold
   C. Humidity   D. Atmospheric pressure

   3.____

4. The Finkelstein Test is the MOST appropriate test for diagnosing what work-related medical condition?
   A. Trigger finger   B. Carpal tunnel
   C. Raynaud's syndrome   D. DeQuervain's syndrome

   4.____

5. Deposition of liquid particles in the respiratory system is dependent on which of the following?
   A. Viscosity   B. Solubility
   C. Particle size   D. Specific gravity

   5.____

6. What layer of the skin is the major barrier for almost all substances, for hydrophilic substances in particular?
   A. Dermis   B. Stratum corneum
   C. Stratum spinosum   D. Stratum granulosum

   6.____

7. Isopropanol metabolizes into what chemical in the human body?
   A. Glucose   B. Acetone   C. Benzene   D. Methanol

   7.____

8. Which of the following are capable of destroying living tissue and have a destructive effect on other substances, especially on combustible materials?
   A. Corrosives   B. Explosives
   C. Radioactive materials   D. Oxidizing materials

   8.____

9. According to the Hearing Conservation Amendment, all cases in which the sound levels exceed what decibel level on an eight-hour time-weighted average, must be administered as continuing, effective hearing conservation program?
   A. 80 dBA   B. 85 dBA   C. 90 dBA   D. 95 dBA

   9.____

10. With what instrument is humidity, or the moisture content of the air, generally measured?   10.____
    A. Barometer   B. Hydrometer
    C. Psychrometer   D. Dry bulb thermometer

11. What bodily function is an important mechanism for increasing body temperature by causing metabolic health production to increase to several times the resting rate?   11.____
    A. Sweating   B. Shivering
    C. Vasodilation   D. Vasoconstriction

12. All of the following types of radioactivity are used routinely in ordinary manufacturing operations EXCEPT   12.____
    A. x-ray   B. beta radiation
    C. alpha radiation   D. neutron radiation

13. When performing air sampling, from what location should samples be taken?   13.____
    A. Ground level   B. Warmest area
    C. Breathing zone   D. Near entryways

14. On what part of the body is the epidermis the thickest?   14.____
    A. Scalp   B. Elbows
    C. Abdomen   D. Soles of the feet

15. Which of the following substances can make skin sensitive to light?   15.____
    A. Nickel   B. Coal tar   C. Poison ivy   D. Chromic acid

16. All of the following are basic requirements of industrial skin cleansers EXCEPT: They should   16.____
    A. easily flow through dispensers
    B. not harmfully dehydrate the skin
    C. be protected against microbial contamination
    D. have an abrasive component to remove industrial soil

17. Which of the following causes the GREATEST percentage of occupational dermatological injuries?   17.____
    A. Abrasions   B. Non-chemical burns
    C. Environmental allergens   D. Lacerations and punctures

18. What type of ionizing radiation is unable to cause an injury to the skin?   18.____
    A. Beta-radiation   B. Gamma-radiation
    C. Alpha-radiation   D. Bremsstrahlung-radiation

19. What type of burn is almost always deep and often extensive, with the type of clothing being a major factor in severity?   19.____
    A. Steam   B. Flame   C. Hot-solid   D. Molten-metal

20. What part of the ear collects sound waves from the air and funnels them into the ear canal to the tympanic membrane?
   A. Auricle
   B. Eardrum
   C. Ear canal
   D. External auditory canal

20.____

21. What part of the ear functions to filter out particulate matter and other large pieces of debris?
   A. Pinna
   B. Cerumen
   C. Vibrissae
   D. Ossicles

21.____

22. Pressure in the eyeball is measured with what instrument?
   A. Phoropter
   B. Barometer
   C. Tonometer
   D. Ohthalmoscope

22.____

23. What is the MOST common form of glaucoma?
   A. Idiopathic glaucoma
   B. Acute-angle closure glaucoma
   C. Primary open-angle glaucoma
   D. Chronic closed-angle glaucoma

23.____

24. What is the MOST common industrial test for visual acuity?
   A. Visual field test
   B. The Snellen Chart
   C. Tonometer reading
   D. Refractive correction

24.____

25. What type of eye protection equipment is sufficient for 90% of general industrial work?
   A. Safety glasses
   B. Splash goggles
   C. Chipping goggles
   D. Phototropic lenses

25.____

KEY (CORRECT ANSWERS)

1.	D		11.	B
2.	D		12.	D
3.	B		13.	C
4.	D		14.	D
5.	C		15.	B
6.	B		16.	D
7.	B		17.	D
8.	A		18.	C
9.	B		19.	B
10.	C		20.	A

21.	C
22.	A
23.	C
24.	B
25.	A

TEST 4

DIRECTIONS: Each question or incomplete statement is followed by several suggested answers or completions. Select the one that BEST answers the question or completes the statement. *PRINT THE LETTER OF THE CORRECT ANSWER IN THE SPACE AT THE RIGHT.*

1. All of the following represent the three spectral bands of radiation emitted during welding processes EXCEPT

    A. visible   B. infrared   C. ionizing   D. ultraviolet

1._____

2. The health effect on a chemical exposure is considered to be acute if it

    A. is irreversible   B. recurs periodically
    C. is relatively short-lived   D. appears within 7 days of exposure

2._____

3. Which of the following substances can be detected by either obtaining a urine sample or a blood sample?

    A. Zinc   B. Nickel
    C. Acetone   D. Ethyl benzene

3.____

4. "Prolonged exposure" is typically defined as what time period?

    A. 5-7 days   B. 7-14 days
    C. 2-6 weeks   D. 3 months or longer

4.____

5. What type of epidemiological data identifies a change in prevalence of disease in a subgroup of a population?

    A. Illustrative   B. Descriptive   C. Prospective   D. Retrospective

5._____

6. For what reason is air monitoring performed?
To measure the

    A. amount of a chemical that has been absorbed via the lungs
    B. total exposure, both on and off the job, to harmful substances
    C. composition of the external environment surrounding the worker
    D. effects of increased work load resulting in increased air intake of the contaminant

6._____

7. Which of the following statements is TRUE regarding irritants and irritation?

    A. Irritants are often grouped according to their site of action.
    B. A primary irritant exerts extensive systemic toxic action.
    C. The degree of local irritation of many liquid irritants is related to their systemic toxicities.
    D. Irritation most frequently results from a direct mechanical reaction with constituents in the tissue.

7._____

8. Which of the following is a formless fluid that completely fills its container and that exerts an equal pressure in all directions?

    A. Gas   B. Mist   C. Fume   D. Vapor

8.____

9.   Vapor pressure is highly dependent on which of the following?   9.____
      A. Solubility   B. Evaporation
      C. Surface area   D. Temperature

10.   Compounds that contain only carbon and hydrogen atoms are referred to as   10.____
      A. isomers   B. amino acids
      C. nucleic acids   D. hydrocarbons

11.   What characteristic of a liquid is the lowest temperature at which it gives   11.____
      off enough vapor to form an ignitable mixture with the air near the surface of
      the liquid?
      A. Reactivity   B. Flash point
      C. Flammability   D. Combustibility

12.   Which of the following chemicals can commonly act as an upper respiratory   12.____
      irritant?
      A. Ozone   B. Phosgene
      C. Sulfuric acid   D. Nitrogen dioxide

13.   What is the MINIMUM percentage of atmospheric oxygen required to   13.____
      support life?
      A. 18%   B. 32%   C. 64%   D. 75%

14.   How does the fire point of a liquid relate to the flash point temperature of a   14.____
      liquid?
      The fire point is usually _____ the flash point.
      A. 10°F below   B. 5°F below
      C. 5°F above   D. 10°F above

15.   Aliphatic compounds take their name from the Greek word *aliphe*, which   15.____
      means
      A. fat   B. water   C. aromatic   D. hazardous

16.   Which of the following substances has the ability to be used as an   16.____
      anesthetic?
      A. Lipophilic solvents   B. Chlorofluorocarbons
      C. Cyclic hydrocarbons   D. Aliphatic hydrocarbons

17.   What is often the PRIMARY factor for the toxicity of a material?   17.____
      A. Size of particles   B. Length of exposure
      C. Number of particles   D. Chemical composition

18.   Which of the following statements is FALSE regarding frequency?   18.____
      A. Frequency is perceived by the human ear as pitch.
      B. The frequency composition of a sound is known as its spectrum.
      C. Broadband noise can be somewhat more harmful than single frequencies.
      D. The audible range of frequencies for humans is between 20 Hz and
          20,000 Hz

19. Which of the following should be included in the general guidelines for
conducting preliminary noise surveys?
   A. The information recorded should cover workers' time-weighted average
exposure.
   B. The survey should define areas where hearing protection will be required.
   C. The information recorded should allow another individual to reproduce the
measured data.
   D. The survey should be carried out in areas where workers within 10 feet of
one another have to shout to communicate.

19.____

20. Most of the damage-risk criteria are written for what type of noise because it
is the easiest to define in terms of amplitude, frequency content, and duration?
   A. Impact noise   B. Cyclical noise
   C. Continuous noise   D. Intermittent noise

20.____

21. Which of the following protective devices can reduce bone-conducted
sound?
   A. Helmets   B. Ear plugs   C. Ear muffs   D. Canal caps

21.____

22. Which of the following statements are TRUE regarding noise-induced
hearing loss?
   A. It can result from direct trauma to the head or ear.
   B. It denotes injury to the sensorineural elements of the inner ear.
   C. It usually affects both ears equally in the extent and degree of loss.
   D. It can result from one or a few exposures to sudden intense acoustic
energy.

22.____

23. What would be the BEST choice of hearing-protective equipment for a
worker who is only exposed to hazardous noise intermittently?
   A. Helmet   B. Ear plugs   C. Ear muffs   D. Canal caps

23.____

24. Which of the following would be a practical manner of measuring the noise
exposure of workers who perform a variety of tasks in various locations?
   A. A noise dosimeter
   B. A sound survey meter
   C. An octave-band analyzer
   D. A tape and graphic level recorder

24.____

25. To what degree can the threshold of hearing vary among healthy
individuals?
   A. ± 10 dB   B. ± 20 dB   C. ±30 dB   D. ± 50 dB

25.____

KEY (CORRECT ANSWERS)

1.	C		11.	B
2.	C		12.	C
3.	C		13.	A
4.	C		14.	C
5.	B		15.	A
6.	C		16.	C
7.	A		17.	D
8.	A		18.	C
9.	D		19.	C
10.	A		20.	C

21.	A
22.	C
23.	C
24.	A
25.	A

EXAMINATION SECTION

TEST 1

DIRECTIONS: Each question or incomplete statement is followed by several suggested answers or completions. Select the one that BEST answers the question or completes the statement. *PRINT THE LETTER OF THE CORRECT ANSWER IN THE SPACE AT THE RIGHT.*

1. What unit is used to measure the rate of radioactive decay?   1.____
   A. Curie   B. Sievert   C. Roentgen   D. Becquerel

2. Alpha-emitters are chemically similar to what substance in their action within   2.____
   the human body?
   A. Iron   B. Water   C. Sodium   D. Calcium

3. Which of the following represents the average annual dose an individual   3.____
   receives from background radiation?
   A. 100 mR/year   B. 200 mR/year
   C. 300 mR/year   D. 400 mR/year

4. Hydrogen-3 is another name for what element?   4.____
   A. Trititum   B. Radium   C. Technetium   D. Plutonium

5. Which of the following areas of the body is the MOST sensitive to the effects   5.____
   of radiation exposure?
   A. Bone   B. Nerve   C. Muscle   D. Bone marrow

6. If you double the distance from the source of radiation, the exposure would   6.____
   be decreased to what percentage of the original amount?
   A. 10%   B. 25%   C. 50%   D. 75%

7. What is the MOST frequent route of entry of radioactive material into the   7.____
   body?
   A. Ingestion   B. Inhalation
   C. Absorption through intact skin   D. Absorption through broken skin

8. What is the MOST common skin effect from infrared and visible light?   8.____
   A. Hair loss   B. Sunburn   C. Wrinkles   D. Melanoma

9. A review of laser accidents show that the majority of laser accidents occur   9.____
   A. during alignment
   B. during initial setup
   C. due to failure of interlocks
   D. due to inadequate engineering controls

10. A pale face, a high pulse rate, and dizziness are signs and symptoms of what medical condition?

    A. Heat stroke   B. Dehydration
    C. Heat syncope   D. Heat exhaustion

10._____

11. If an employee experiences what percentage loss of body weight during a work shift, they are likely to be dehydrated?

    A. 0.5%   B. 1.0%   C. 1.5%   D. 2.0%

11._____

12. A burning sensation, blisters, and tingling are signs and symptoms of what medical condition?

    A. Frostbite   B. Carpal tunnel
    C. Raynaud's disorder   D. Diabetic neuropathy

12._____

13. All of the following are engineering controls for cold stress EXCEPT:

    A. Requiring gloves to be worn at temps below -17°C (1°F)
    B. Redesigning equipment to make it safe to use below 2°C (36°F)
    C. Providing hand warming for fine hand work below 16°C (61°F)
    D. Adjusting ventilation to maintain workers' core temperatures at 36°C (96.8°F)

13._____

14. Faintness and blurred vision are signs and symptoms of what medical condition?

    A. Heat stroke   B. Dehydration
    C. Heat syncope   D. Heat exhaustion

14._____

15. If the average heart rate over an eight hour day is greater than _____ bpm, the work and heat stress may be excessive.

    A. 80   B. 90   C. 100   D. 110

15._____

16. What medical condition should be handled as a precursor to heat exhaustion?

    A. Heat rash   B. Heat cramps
    C. Dehydration   D. Heat syncope

16._____

17. Vascular disease can be a factor in all of the following medical conditions EXCEPT

    A. frostbite   B. chilblains
    C. hypothermia   D. Raynaud's disorder

17._____

18. A worker's manual dexterity begins to decrease after 10-20 minutes of uninterrupted work in temperatures below what point?

    A. 15°C (59°F)   B. 16°C (61°F)   C. 17°C (63°F)   D. 18°C (64°F)

18._____

19. The _____ nervous system includes the cranial and spinal nerves.

    A. central   B. somatic   C. peripheral   D. autonomic

19._____

20. Control of voluntary movements, sensory experience, abstract thought, memory, learning, and consciousness is located in what area of the brain?

    A. Cortex   B. Cerebrum   C. Cerebellum   D. Basal ganglia

20._____

21. Under optimal conditions, simple auditory, visual, and tactile reactions times are about how many seconds?

    A. 0.2   B. 0.5   C. 0.8   D. 1.2

21._____

22. All of the following functions are addressed by the field of biomechanics EXCEPT

    A. body posture   B. range of motion
    C. mental processes   D. muscle strength

22._____

23. Which of the following worker populations reported the HIGHEST incidence ratio for compensation claims due to back injuries?

    A. Nurses   B. Material handlers
    C. Garbage collectors   D. Construction workers

23._____

24. In general, women have approximately what percentage of the physical strength as a man?

    A. 25%   B. 50%   C. 66%   D. 75%

24._____

25. _____ permits the operator to modify the work environment and equipment so that it conforms to the individual's particular set of characteristics as well as to subjective preferences.

    A. Flexibility   B. Adaptability
    C. Adjustability   D. Comfortability

25._____

KEY (CORRECT ANSWERS)

1.	D		11.	C
2.	D		12.	A
3.	C		13.	A
4.	A		14.	C
5.	D		15.	D
6.	B		16.	C
7.	D		17.	C
8.	B		18.	B
9.	A		19.	C
10.	D		20.	B

21.	A
22.	C
23.	D
24.	C
25.	C

TEST 2

1. What medical condition is the result of compression of the ulnar nerve below the notch of the elbow?
   A. Epicondylitis
   B. Carpal tunnel syndrome
   C. Cubital tunnel syndrome
   D. DeQuervain's syndrome

   1._____

2. What medical condition is a special case of tendosynovitis where the tendon becomes nearly locked so that its forced movement is not smooth but snaps or jerks?
   A. Trigger finger
   B. Carpal tunnel syndrome
   C. Cubital tunnel syndrome
   D. DeQuervain's syndrome

   2._____

3. Which of the following is a small, flat, synovia-filled sac lined with a slippery cushion that prevents rubbing of a muscle or tendon against bone?
   A. Bursa   B. Tendon   C. Ligament   D. Cartilage

   3._____

4. The term _____ implies complete elimination or destruction of all forms of microbial life.
   A. disinfection
   B. sterilization
   C. pasteurization
   D. decontamination

   4._____

5. In which of the following are viroids able to cause disease?
   A. Fish   B. Birds   C. Plants   D. Humans

   5._____

6. Which of the following statements is TRUE regarding zoonotic diseases? They are diseases
   A. that are limited to animals
   B. that are acquired from spores
   C. that affect both humans and animals
   D. common to wild animals in captivity

   6._____

7. What is the MOST common chronic blood-borne infection in the United States?
   A. HIV   B. Malaria   C. Hepatitis B   D. Hepatitis C

   7._____

8. What percentage of the world's population remains affected by tuberculosis?
   A. 10%   B. 25%   C. 33%   D. 50%

   8._____

9. Other than Legionnaires' disease, what medical condition is a clinical and epidemiological distinct manifestation of legionellosis?
   A. Hantavirus   B. Salmonella   C. Shigellosis   D. Pontiac fever

   9._____

10. Which of the following is the MOST effective method of cleaning dry, dusty materials without producing excessive amounts of airborne contaminants?
    A. Vacuuming
    B. Wet mopping
    C. Steam cleaning
    D. Using compressed air

10.____

11. Which of the following statements is FALSE regarding personal monitoring?
    A. Personal monitoring can be conducted during employee breaks.
    B. Personal monitoring is usually performed during a specific time period.
    C. It is important to interview an individual before, during, and after personal monitoring.
    D. Personal monitoring measures the ambient air concentration of a substance in a given area.

11.____

12. When a contaminant is released into the atmosphere as a dust, mist, or fume, its concentration can be expressed in all of the following ways EXCEPT
    A. ppm
    B. gcf
    C. $\mu g/m^3$
    D. $oz/1,000\ ft^3$

12.____

13. If after analysis a sampling result is less than the permissible exposure limit (PEL), what can be determined?
    It should
    A. be interpreted as a clean bill of health
    B. be considered to be in compliance with the law
    C. guarantee that the workplace is safe for employees
    D. be deemed adequate to protect employees from multiple exposures

13.____

14. Which of the following, also referred to as ceiling levels, are used to evaluate brief exposure times or peak releases?
    A. Time-weighted average (TWA)
    B. Short term exposure limit (STEL)
    C. Recommended exposure limit (REL)
    D. Threshold value limit (TLV)

14.____

15. Which of the following statements are TRUE regarding chemical inventories?
    A. They identify the chemical hazards that are present in a process.
    B. They specify the quantities of chemical used in various processes.
    C. They classify the degree of risk from exposure to the chemicals listed.
    D. They indicate a point in a process at which employees risk being exposed.

15.____

16. Which of the following statements are TRUE regarding biological monitoring?
    A. The results of biological monitoring must be reproducible.
    B. Biological is not limited to variability among individuals.
    C. Laboratory reliability does not affect the outcome of biological monitoring.
    D. The significance of result from biological monitoring is never open to interpretation.

16.____

17. Which of the following anomalies may affect precision?
    A. Method error
    B. Incorrect calculations
    C. Poorly calibrated equipment
    D. Intraday concentration fluctuations

17.____

18. According to TLV® guidelines, short-term exposures may exceed how many times the TLV® for no more than a total of 30 minutes during the workday?
    A. 1.5 times   B. 2.0 times   C. 2.5 times   D. 3.0 times

18.____

19. Which of the following is the MOST commonly used solid sorbent?
    A. Silica gel   B. Porous polymers
    C. Molecular sieves   D. Activated charcoal

19.____

20. What is the MOST commonly used filter for aerosol samples?
    A. Membrane filters
    B. Electrostatic filters
    C. Glass and quartz filters
    D. Polycarbonate straight pore filters

20.____

21. Which of the following absorption devices is easiest to use?
    A. Fritted bubblers   B. Spiral absorbers
    C. Helical absorbers   D. Gas wash bottles

21.____

22. Respirable particles are those that are retained in the lung and are generally considered to be of aerodynamic size below 10μm.
    What device would be used to collect particles of respirable size?
    A. Cyclone   B. Impinger
    C. Elutriator   D. Electrostatic precipitator

22.____

23. What device can be used to determine particle size distribution?
    A. Elutriator   B. Suction pump
    C. Inertial impactor   D. Electrostatic precipitator

23.____

24. What device, which consists of a large tube through which the direction of airflow is opposite to the direction of gravity, is commonly used for cotton dust sampling?
    A. Impinger   B. Inertial impactor
    C. Vertical elutriator   D. Horizontal elutriator

24.____

25. Which of the following would be an example of a primary calibration device?
    A. Rotameter   B. Dry test meter
    C. Wet test meter   D. Soap bubble meter

25.____

KEY (CORRECT ANSWERS)

1.	C		11.	D
2.	A		12.	A
3.	A		13.	B
4.	B		14.	B
5.	C		15.	A
6.	C		16.	A
7.	D		17.	D
8.	C		18.	D
9.	D		19.	D
10.	A		20.	A

21.	D
22.	D
23.	C
24.	C
25.	D

TEST 3

DIRECTIONS: Each question or incomplete statement is followed by several suggested answers or completions. Select the one that BEST answers the question or completes the statement. *PRINT THE LETTER OF THE CORRECT ANSWER IN THE SPACE AT THE RIGHT.*

1. OSHA Standard 29 CFR 1910.20, Access to Employee Exposure and Medical Records, requires that employee exposure records be kept for how many years?

   A. 5   B. 7   C. 12   D. 30   1.____

2. Background data of air sampling, such as lab reports and field notes, should be retained for how many years?

   A. 1   B. 3   C. 5   D. 7   2.____

3. When a facility is brought online, it is recommended that the ventilation system be operating for what time period prior to occupancy to purge construction-related contaminants?

   A. 12 hours   B. 24 hours   C. 36 hours   D. 48 hours   3.____

4. The direct flow of chemicals through seams, pinholes, or closures is referred to as

   A. infiltration   B. penetration   C. permeation   D. annihilation   4.____

5. Which of the following can be an appropriate solution for infrequent emergencies or non-routine events?   5.____
   A. Engineering controls
   B. Executive controls
   C. Administrative controls
   D. Personal protective equipment

6. All of the following are acceptable control methods for reducing environmental hazards EXCEPT   6.____
   A. job rotation
   B. dry work methods
   C. good housekeeping
   D. local exhaust ventilation

7. Which of the following methods is likely the EASIEST method to prevent hazardous physical contact?   7.____
   A. Providing remote controls for equipment
   B. Isolating equipment such as hot water lines
   C. Automating processes to eliminate worker exposure
   D. Isolating workers by enclosing them in control booths

8. A test subject may not eat, drink, smoke, or chew gum for what time period before a saccharin solution aerosol fit test procedure?   8.____
   A. 15 minutes   B. 30 minutes   C. 1 hour   D. 2 hours

9. According to AAOHN recommendations, service industries should have one full-time occupational health nurse for every _____ employees.   9.____
   A. 500   B. 750   C. 1,000   D. 1,500

10. In what percentage of companies is the occupational health nurse the sole health care provider at the worksite?

    A. 15%   B. 30%   C. 50%   D. 75%

10._____

11. OSHA schedules inspections on a priority system. Which of the following events has the LOWEST priority?

    A. In response to fatalities
    B. In response to employee complaints
    C. Random inspection of high hazard industries
    D. In response to multiple hospitalization incidents

11._____

12. Congress has instructed OSHA that, exclusive of serious violations, it must find more than how many other violations before any penalty can be imposed against a company?

    A. 1   B. 5   C. 10   D. 15

12._____

13. What is the structure that guards the opening of the trachea?

    A. Uvula   B. Larynx   C. Pharynx   D. Epiglottis

13._____

14. What does the term *spirometry* refer to?

    A. Rate of respiration during exertion
    B. Measurement of carbon dioxide in tissues
    C. Pressure equalization across a permeable membrane
    D. Measurement of air (ventilator capacity of the lungs)

14._____

15. What is the typical vital capacity of the lungs?

    A. 1-2 liters   B. 2-3 liters   C. 3-4 liters   D. 4-5 liters

15._____

16. Which of the following helps to prevent contact with acids, alkalis, and some types of metallic acids?

    A. Vanishing cream   B. Water-repellent cream
    C. Solvent-repellant cream   D. Alcohol-based hand sanitizers

16._____

17. The skin is the chief rate-limiting barrier against which of the following substances?

    A. Gases   B. Alkalis
    C. Organic solvents   D. Aqueous solutions

17._____

18. What is another name for the external auditory canal?

    A. Pinna   B. Meatus
    C. Vibrissae   D. Eustachian tube

18._____

19. The ossicles connect the eardrum to an opening in the wall of the inner ear called the

    A. cochlea   B. semicircular canals
    C. fenesrtra vestibule   D. fenestra rotundum

19._____

20. What is the common term for the sclera portion of the eye?　　　　　　20.____
    A. Lower lid　　　　　　　　　　B. Eyelashes
    C. Tear gland　　　　　　　　　　D. White of the eye

21. What is the name of the circular aperture that is formed by the iris of the　　21.____
eye?
    A. Lens　　　　　B. Pupil　　　　　C. Retina　　　　　D. Cornea

22. What is the function of the tarsal glands of the eye?　　　　　　22.____
    A. To increase the focus of eyesight
    B. To protect the eye from dust and other particles
    C. To rid the eye of foreign particles
    D. To lubricate the eyeball and eyelid

23. All of the following may be classified as simple asphyxiants EXCEPT　　23.____
    A. nitrogen　　　　　　　　　　B. hydrogen
    C. methane　　　　　　　　　　D. carbon monoxide

24. For what reason is the aerodynamic equivalent diameter of a particle　　24.____
important?
    A. It indicates toxicity levels.
    B. It is necessary for compliance with OSHA's permissible exposure limits.
    C. It helps to determine what type of personal protective equipment is
       needed.
    D. It determines where in the respiratory tract the particle is most likely to be
       deposited.

25. For cancer and genetic effects, the limiting value is specified in terms of a　　25.____
derived quantity called the effective dose equivalent.
The effective dose equivalent received in any year by an adult worker should
NOT exceed what threshold?
    A. 2 rem　　　　　B. 5 rem　　　　　C. 7 rem　　　　　D. 10 rem

KEY (CORRECT ANSWERS)

1.	D		11.	C
2.	A		12.	C
3.	D		13.	D
4.	B		14.	D
5.	D		15.	C
6.	B		16.	B
7.	B		17.	D
8.	A		18.	B
9.	B		19.	C
10.	C		20.	D

21.	B
22.	D
23.	C
24.	D
25.	B

TEST 4

DIRECTIONS: Each question or incomplete statement is followed by several suggested answers or completions. Select the one that BEST answers the question or completes the statement. *PRINT THE LETTER OF THE CORRECT ANSWER IN THE SPACE AT THE RIGHT.*

1. Particle that are 10 µm or larger are removed by what area of the respiratory system?
   A. Tracheal region
   B. Bronchial region
   C. Alveolar region
   D. Nose and upper airways

   1.____

2. Medium size particles, between 5 µm and 10 µm, are captured by what area of the respiratory system?
   A. Tracheal region
   B. Bronchial region
   C. Alveolar region
   D. Nose and upper airways

   2.____

3. Small particles, between 0.5 µm and 3 µm, are small enough to enter what region of the respiratory system?
   A. Tracheal region
   B. Bronchial region
   C. Alveolar region
   D. Nose and upper airways

   3.____

4. Occupational health nurses must move through several steps sequentially in order to solve problems. Which of the following is the PROPER order?
   A. Evaluation, anticipation, recognition, control
   B. Anticipation, recognition, evaluation, control
   C. Recognition, anticipation, evaluation, control
   D. Anticipation, evaluation, recognition, control

   4.____

5. For any given chemical, a high LD_{50} value generally means
   A. low toxicity
   B. high toxicity
   C. carcinogenicity
   D. teratogenicity

   5.____

6. General ventilation is also referred to as _____ ventilation.
   A. point   B. dilution   C. workplace   D. secondary

   6.____

7. Which of the following is the MOST appropriate definition of "noise"?
   A. Any loud sound
   B. Any unwanted sound
   C. Any sound above the prescribed
   D. Any level of sound harmful to the human ear

   7.____

8. The nucleus of an atom contains positively charged particles called
   A. prions   B. protons   C. positrons   D. electrons

   8.____

9. Beta particles have the ability to penetrate how deep into the human body?
   A. 0.1-0.5 inches
   B. 0.5-1.0 inches
   C. 1.0-1.5 inches
   D. 1.5-2.0 inches

   9.____

10. All of the following are forms of non-ionizing radiation EXCEPT
    A. visible light
    B. gamma radiation
    C. ultraviolet radiation
    D. microwave radiation

10._____

11. What is the normal rectal temperature for a human being measured in degrees centigrade?
    A. 37.6   B. 37.8   C. 38.0   D. 38.2

11._____

12. In what area of the body would chilblains be found?
    A. On the eyelids
    B. On the feet
    C. On the fingers
    D. On the palms of the hands

12._____

13. Which of the following is an occupational disease that is caused by a fungus?
    A. Eysipelas
    B. Lyme disease
    C. Tuberculosis
    D. Histoplasmosis

13._____

14. Tuberculosis is called by what type of biological hazard?
    A. Prions   B. Virus   C. Fungus   D. Bacteria

14._____

15. Legionnaires' disease is a type of what medical condition?
    A. Asthma   B. Influenza   C. Pneumonia   D. Emphysema

15._____

16. Which of the following, also known as prickly heat or heat rash, is an occupational skin disease related to heat and sweat?
    A. Eczema   B. Psoriasis   C. Miliaria   D. Urticaria

16._____

17. The medical condition, hyperopia, is MOST commonly referred to as
    A. glaucoma
    B. color blindness
    C. farsightedness
    D. nearsightedness

17._____

18. What is the MAJOR symptom associated with rod monochromatism?
    A. Glaucoma
    B. Color blindness
    C. Farsightedness
    D. Nearsightedness

18._____

19. If inhaled gases are fat soluble and not metabolized, what bodily system clears these gases from the body?
    A. Endocrine
    B. Urinary
    C. Respiratory
    D. Gastrointestinal

19._____

20. Cryogenic fluids pose several safety concerns including frostbite. Liquid _____ is the MOST common cryogenic liquid found in the workplace.
    A. neon   B. argon   C. helium   D. nitrogen

20._____

21. When temperatures fall below _____, steps should be taken to implement workplace monitoring.
    A. 15°C (59°F)
    B. 16°C (61°F)
    C. 17°C (63°F)
    D. 18°C (64°F)

21._____

22. Which of the following is operationally defined as a reduced muscular ability to continue an existing effort?
    A. Sprain   B. Strain   C. Fatigue   D. Cramp

22.____

23. _____ is defined as an invasion on the body by pathogenic microorganisms and the reaction of the tissues to their presence and to the toxins generated by them.
    A. Immunity   B. Infection   C. Virulence   D. Pathogenicity

23.____

24. According to indoor air quality rules proposed by OSHA, carbon monoxide levels in places of employment must be kept below a level of _____ ppm.
    A. 600   B. 700   C. 800   D. 900

24.____

25. Fit testing should be conducted how often on all employees required to wear tight-fitting respirators?
    A. Every 2 months   B. Every 4 months
    C. Every 6 months   D. Every 12 months

25.____

KEY (CORRECT ANSWERS)

1.	D		11.	A	
2.	A		12.	B	
3.	C		13.	D	
4.	B		14.	D	
5.	A		15.	C	
6.	B		16.	C	
7.	D		17.	C	
8.	B		18.	B	
9.	A		19.	C	
10.	B		20.	D	

21.	B
22.	C
23.	B
24.	C
25.	D

EXAMINATION SECTION
TEST 1

DIRECTIONS: Each question or incomplete statement is followed by several suggested
answers or completions. Select the one that BEST answers the question or
completes the statement. *PRINT THE LETTER OF THE CORRECT ANSWER
IN THE SPACE AT THE RIGHT.*

1. The MOST common cause of death before age 65 is

    A. cerebrovascular disease   B. malignant neoplasm
    C. heart disease   D. diabetes mellitus
    E. liver cirrhosis

1.____

2. Of the following, the disease NOT transmitted by mosquitoes is

    A. dengue fever
    B. lymphocytic choriomeningitis
    C. western equine encephalitis
    D. St. Louis encephalitis
    E. yellow fever

2.____

3. The single MOST effective measure to prevent hookworm infection is

    A. washing hands
    B. washing clothes daily
    C. cooking food at high temperatures
    D. wearing shoes
    E. none of the above

3.____

4. Transmission of tuberculosis in the United States occurs MOST often by

    A. fomites   B. blood transfusion
    C. inhalation of droplet   D. transplacentally
    E. milk

4.____

5. The second MOST common cause of death in the United States is

    A. accident   B. cancer
    C. cerebrovascular disease   D. heart disease
    E. AIDS

5.____

6. All of the following bacteria are spread through fecal-oral transmission EXCEPT

    A. haemophilus influenza type B   B. campylobacter
    C. escherichia coli   D. salmonella
    E. shigella

6.____

7. Routine immunization is particularly important for children in day care because pre-
school-aged children currently have the highest age specific incidence of all of the following EXCEPT

    A. H-influenzae type B   B. neisseria meningitis
    C. measles   D. rubella
    E. pertussis

7.____

8. Hand washing and masks are necessary for physical contact with all of the following patients EXCEPT

    A. lassa fever   B. diphtheria
    C. coxsackie virus disease   D. varicella
    E. plaque

8.____

9. Control measures for prevention of tick-borne infections include all of the following EXCEPT:

    A. Tick-infested area should be avoided whenever possible.
    B. If a tick-infested area is entered, protective clothing that covers the arms, legs, and other exposed area should be worn.
    C. Tick/insect repellent should be applied to the skin.
    D. Ticks should be removed promptly.
    E. Daily inspection of pets and removal of ticks is not indicated.

9.____

10. The PRINCIPAL reservoir of giardia lamblia infection is

    A. humans   B. mosquitoes   C. rodents
    D. sandflies   E. cats

10.____

11. Most community-wide epidemics of giardia lamblia infection result from

    A. inhalation of droplets
    B. eating infected meats
    C. eating contaminated eggs
    D. drinking contaminated water
    E. blood transfusions

11.____

12. Epidemics of giardia lamblia occurring in day care centers are USUALLY caused by

    A. inhalation of droplets
    B. person-to-person contact
    C. fecal and oral contact
    D. eating contaminated food
    E. all of the above

12.____

13. Measures of the proportion of the population exhibiting a phenomenon at a particular time is called the

    A. incidence   B. prevalence
    C. prospective study   D. cohort study
    E. all of the above

13.____

14. The occurrence of an event or characteristic over a period of time is called

    A. incidence   B. prevalence
    C. specificity   D. case control study
    E. cohort study

14.____

15. All of the following are live attenuated viral vaccines EXCEPT

    A. measles   B. mumps
    C. rubella   D. rabies
    E. yellow fever

15.____

16. Chlorinating air-cooling towers can prevent 16.____

    A. scarlet fever   B. impetigo
    C. typhoid fever   D. mycobacterium tuberculosis
    E. legionnaire's disease

17. Eliminating the disease causing agent may be done by all of the following methods 17.____
EXCEPT

    A. chemotherapeutic   B. cooling
    C. heating   D. chlorinating
    E. disinfecting

18. Which of the following medications is used to eliminate pharyngeal carriage of neisseria 18.____
meningitidis?

    A. Penicillin   B. Rifampin
    C. Isoniazid   D. Erythromycin
    E. Gentamicin

19. Post-exposure prophylaxis is recommended for rabies after the bite of all of the following 19.____
animals EXCEPT

    A. chipmunks   B. skunks   C. raccoons
    D. bats   E. foxes

20. To destroy the spores of clostridium botulinum, canning requires a temperature of AT 20.____
LEAST _____°C.

    A. 40   B. 60   C. 80   D. 100   E. 120

21. All of the following are killed or fractionated vaccines EXCEPT 21.____

    A. hepatitis B   B. yellow fever
    C. H-influenza type B   D. pneumococcus
    E. rabies

22. Of the following, the disease NOT spreadly by food is 22.____

    A. typhoid fever   B. shigellosis
    C. typhus   D. cholera
    E. legionellosis

23. In the United States, the HIGHEST attack rate of sheigella infection occurs in children 23.____
between _____ of age.

    A. 1 to 6 months   B. 6 months to 1 year
    C. 1 to 4 years   D. 6 to 10 years
    E. 10 to 15 years

24. Risk factors for cholera include all of the following EXCEPT 24.____

    A. occupational exposure
    B. lower socioeconomic
    C. unsanitary condition
    D. high socioeconomic
    E. high population density in low income areas

25. The MOST common cause of traveler's diarrhea is
    A. escherichia coli
    C. salmonella
    E. campalobacter
    B. shigella
    D. cholera

25.____

_____

KEY (CORRECT ANSWERS)

1.	C		11.	D
2.	B		12.	B
3.	D		13.	B
4.	C		14.	A
5.	B		15.	D
6.	A		16.	E
7.	B		17.	B
8.	C		18.	B
9.	E		19.	A
10.	A		20.	E

21. B
22. C
23. C
24. D
25. A

_____

TEST 2

DIRECTIONS: Each question or incomplete statement is followed by several suggested answers or completions. Select the one that BEST answers the question or completes the statement. *PRINT THE LETTER OF THE CORRECT ANSWER IN THE SPACE AT THE RIGHT.*

1. The increased prevalence of entamoeba histolytica infection results from   1._____

    A. lower socioeconomic status in endemic area
    B. institutionalized (especially mentally retarded) population
    C. immigrants from endemic area
    D. promiscuous homosexual men
    E. all of the above

2. The MOST common infection acquired in the hospital is _____ infection.   2._____

    A. surgical wound   B. lower respiratory tract
    C. urinary tract   D. bloodstream
    E. gastrointestinal

3. The etiologic agent of Rocky Mountain spotted fever is   3._____

    A. rickettsia prowazekii   B. rickettsia rickettsii
    C. rickettsia akari   D. coxiella burnetii
    E. rochalimaena quintana

4. The annual death rate for injuries per 100,000 in both sexes is HIGHEST in those _____ years of age.   4._____

    A. 1 to 10   B. 10 to 20   C. 30 to 40
    D. 50 to 60   E. 80 to 90

5. The death rate per 100,000 population due to motor vehicle accident is HIGHEST among   5._____

    A. whites   B. blacks
    C. Asians   D. native Americans
    E. Spanish surnamed

6. Among the following, the HIGHEST rate of homicide occurs in   6._____

    A. whites   B. blacks
    C. native Americans   D. Asians
    E. Spanish surnamed

7. All of the following are true statements regarding coronary heart disease EXCEPT: 7._____

    A. About 4.6 million Americans have coronary heart disease.
    B. Men have a greater risk of MI and sudden death.
    C. Women have a greater risk of angina pectoris.
    D. 25% of coronary heart disease death occurs in individuals under the age of 65 years.
    E. White women have a greater risk of MI and sudden death.

8. Major risk factors for coronary heart disease include all of the following EXCEPT 8._____

   A. smoking
   B. elevated blood pressure
   C. obesity
   D. high level of serum cholesterol
   E. family history of coronary heart disease

9. The MOST common cancer in American men is 9._____

   A. stomach   B. lung   C. leukemia
   D. prostate   E. skin

10. The HIGHEST incidence of prostate cancer occurs in _____ Americans. 10._____

   A. white   B. black   C. Chinese
   D. Asian   E. Spanish

11. All of the following are risk factors for cervical cancer EXCEPT 11._____

   A. smoking
   B. low socioeconomic condition
   C. first coital experience after age 20
   D. multiple sexual partners
   E. contracting a sexually transmitted disease

12. All of the following are independent adverse prognostic factors for lung cancer EXCEPT 12._____

   A. female sex
   B. short duration of symptom
   C. small cell histology
   D. metastatic disease at time of diagnosis
   E. persistently elevated CEA

13. Assuming vaccines with 80% efficacy were available in limited quantity, which vaccine 13._____
    among the following should be given to a military recruit?

   A. Polio   B. Pseudomonas
   C. Meningococcus   D. Influenza
   E. None of the above

14. Among the following, the vaccine which should be administered to children with sickle 14._____
    cell disease is

   A. influenza   B. meningococcus
   C. pseudomonas   D. pneumococcal
   E. yellow fever

15. All of the following are correct statements concerning gastric carcinoma in the United 15._____
    States EXCEPT:

   A. The risk for males is 2.2 times greater than for females.
   B. The incidence is increased.
   C. The risk is higher in persons with pernicious anemia than for the general population.

D. City dwellers have an increased risk of stomach cancer.
E. Workers with high levels of exposure to nickle and rubber are at increased risk.

16. During the first year of life, a condition that can be detected by screening is

    16._____

  A. hypothyroidism
  B. RH incompatibility
  C. phenylketonuria
  D. congenital dislocation of the hip
  E. all of the above

17. The major reservoir of the spread of tuberculosis within a hospital is through

    17._____

  A. patients
  B. custodial staff
  C. doctors
  D. nursing staff
  E. undiagnosed cases

18. All of the following statements are true regarding tuberculosis EXCEPT:

    18._____

  A. Droplet nuclei are the major vehicle for the spread of tuberculosis infection.
  B. The highest incidence is among white Americans.
  C. There is a higher incidence of tuberculosis in prison than in the general population.
  D. HIV infection is a significant independent risk factor for the development of tuberculosis.
  E. A single tubercle bacillus, once having gained access to the terminal air spaces, could establish infection.

19. The human papiloma virus is associated with

    19._____

  A. kaposi sarcoma
  B. hepatoma
  C. cervical neoplasia
  D. nasopharyngeal carcinoma
  E. none of the above

20. General recommendations for prevention of sexually transmitted diseases include all of the following EXCEPT

    20._____

  A. contact tracing
  B. disease reporting
  C. barrier methods
  D. prophylactic antibiotic use
  E. patient education

21. Syphilis remains an important sexually transmitted disease because of all of the following EXCEPT its

    21._____

  A. public health heritage
  B. effect on perinatal morbidity and mortality
  C. association with HIV transmission
  D. escalating rate among black teenagers
  E. inability to be prevented

22. Which of the following statements about homicide is NOT true? Approximately

    A. forty percent are committed by friends and acquaintances
    B. twenty percent is committed by spouse
    C. fifteen percent is committed by a member of the victim's family
    D. fifteen percent is committed by strangers
    E. fifteen percent are labeled *relationship unknown*

22.____

23. Conditions for which screening has proven cost-effective include

    A. phenylketonuria   B. iron deficiency anemia
    C. lead poisoning   D. tuberculosis
    E. all of the above

23.____

24. Suicide is MOST common among

    A. whites   B. blacks
    C. hispanics   D. Asians
    E. none of the above

24.____

25. The MOST frequenty used method of suicide is

    A. hanging   B. poisoning by gases
    C. firearms   D. drug overdose
    E. drowning

25.____

KEY (CORRECT ANSWERS)

1.	E	11.	C
2.	C	12.	A
3.	B	13.	C
4.	E	14.	D
5.	D	15.	B
6.	B	16.	E
7.	E	17.	E
8.	C	18.	B
9.	D	19.	C
10.	B	20.	D

21.	E
22.	B
23.	E
24.	A
25.	C

EXAMINATION SECTION
TEST 1

DIRECTIONS: Each question or incomplete statement is followed by several suggested answers or completions. Select the one that BEST answers the question or completes the statement. *PRINT THE LETTER OF THE CORRECT ANSWER IN THE SPACE AT THE RIGHT.*

1. _____ accounts for the LARGEST percentage of personal health care expenditures in the United States.
   - A. Physician services
   - B. Hospital care
   - C. Nursing homes
   - D. Drug and medical supplies
   - E. Dentist services

   1._____

2. MOST health care expenses in the United States are paid by
   - A government programs
   - B. Medicare
   - B. Medicaid
   - D. private health insurance
   - E. out-of-pocket payments

   2._____

3. A physician is NOT legally required to report
   - A. births and deaths
   - B. suspected child abuse
   - C. gunshot wounds
   - D. a child with croup
   - E. a child with shigella dysentery

   3._____

4. Diseases more likely to occur in blacks than whites include all of the following EXCEPT
   - A. thalassemia
   - B. sickle cell disease
   - C. sarcoidosis
   - D. tuberculosis
   - E. hypertension

   4._____

5. Among the United States population, what malignant tumor has the greatest incidence?
   - A. Breast
   - B. Prostate
   - C. Lung
   - D. Colon
   - E. Stomach

   5._____

6. The MOST frequent cause of chronic obstructive pulmonary disease is

   - A. frequent upper respiratory infection
   - B. smoking
   - C. family member with asthma
   - D. drug abuse
   - E. infantile paralysis

   6._____

7. The ultimate legal responsibility for quality of medical care provided in the hospital rests upon the
   - A. hospital administrator
   - B. chief of nursing staff
   - C. director of the hospital
   - D. principal nurse
   - E. patient's physician

   7._____

8. Routine screening for diabetes is recommended for all patients EXCEPT those with
    A. family history of diabetes
    B. glucose abnormalities associated with pregnancy
    C. marked obesity
    D. an episode of hypoglycemia as a newborn
    E. physical abnormality, such as circulatory dysfunction and frank vascular impairment

9. Low maternal AFP level is associated with
    A. spina bifida   B. Down syndrome
    C. meningocele   D. hypothyroidism
    E. Niemann Pick disease

10. All of the following are skin disorders EXCEPT
    A. psoriasis   B. eczema
    C. scleroderma   D. gout
    E. shingles

11. All of the following are true statements regarding osteoporosis EXCEPT:

    A. The reduction of bone mass in osteoporosis causes the bone to be susceptible to fracture.
    B. Bone loss occurs with advancing age in both men and women.
    C. In developing countries, high parity has been associated with decreased bone mass and increased risk of fracture.
    D. Thin women are at higher risk than obese women.
    E. Daughters of women with osteoporosis tend to have lower bone mass than other women of their age.

12. The MOST common type of occupational disease is
    A. hearing loss   B. dermatitis
    B. pneumoconiosis   D. pulmonary fibrosis
    E. none of the above

13. The incidence of Down syndrome in the United States is about 1 in _____ births.

    A. 700   B. 1200   C. 1500   D. 2000   E. 10000

14. Lyme disease and Rocky Mountain spotted fever CANNOT be prevented by
    A. door and window screen use
    B. hand washing
    C. wearing protective clothing
    D. using insect repellent
    E. immediate tick removal

15. Individuals with egg allergies can be safely administered all of the following vaccines EXCEPT
    A. MMR (Measles-Mumps-Rubella)
    B. hepatitis B
    C. influenza
    D. DTaP (Diphtheria-Tetanus-Whooping Cough)
    E. none of the above

16. Lifetime prevalence of cocaine use is HIGHER among
    A. Hispanics   B. blacks   C. whites   D. Asians
    E. none of the above

17. The effectiveness of preventive measures against chronic illness is BEST determined   17._____
from trends in
    A. incidence   B. mortality   C. prevalence   D. frequency of complication
    E. all of the above

18. Primary prevention of congenital heart disease includes all of the following established   18._____
measures EXCEPT:
    A. Genetic counseling of potential parents and families with congenital heart disease
    B. Avoidance of exposure to viral diseases during pregnancy
    C. Avoidance of all vaccines to all children which eliminate the reservoir of infection
    D. Avoidance of radiation during pregnancy
    E. Avoidance of exposure during first trimester of pregnancy to gas fumes, air pollution,
       cigarettes, alcohol

19. All of the following are true statements regarding genetic factors associated with   19._____
congenital heart disease EXCEPT:
    A. The offspring of a parent with a congenital heart disease has a malformation rate
       ranging from 1.4% to 16.1%.
    B. Identical twins are both affected 25 to 30% of the time.
    C. Single gene disorder accounts for less than 1% of all cardiac congenital anomalies.
    D. Environment does not play a role in cardiac anomalies
    E. Other finding of familial aggregation suggests polygenic factors.

20. MOST likely inadequately supplied in strict vegetarian adults is   20._____
    A. vitamin A   B. thiamin   C. vitamin B_{12} D. niacin   E. protein

21. The MOST common reservoir of acquired immune deficiency syndrome is   21._____

    A. humans   B. mosquitoes   C. cats   D. dogs   E. monkeys

22. A definitive indicator of active tuberculosis is   22._____
    A. chronic persistent cough
    B. positive PPD
    C. night sweats
    D. positive sputum test
    E. hilar adenopathy on chest x-ray

23. Which of the following is NOT a risk factor for development of colorectal carcinoma?   23._____
    A. Familial polyposis coli   B. Furcot's syndrome
    C. High fiber diet   D. Increased dietary fat
    E. Villous polyps

24. According to the American Cancer Society, starting at the age of 50, men and women at   24._____
average risk for developing colorectal cancer should follow which of the following
screening regimens?
    A. Colonoscopy every ten years
    B. Flexible sigmoidoscopy every two years
    C. Double-contrast barium enema every two years
    D. CT colonography (virtual colonoscopy) every year
    E. None of the above

25. The MOST common malignancy among women is of the   25._____
    A. lung   B. breast   C. ovary   D. rectum   E. vagina

KEY (CORRECT ANSWERS)

1.	B		11.	C
2.	D		12.	A
3.	D		13.	A
4.	A		14.	B
5.	D		15.	C
6.	B		16.	C
7.	E		17.	C
8.	D		18.	C
9.	B		19.	D
10.	D		20.	C

21. A
22. D
23. C
24. A
25. B

TEST 2

DIRECTIONS: Each question or incomplete statement is followed by several suggested answers or completions. Select the one that BEST answers the question or completes the statement. *PRINT THE LETTER OF THE CORRECT ANSWER IN THE SPACE AT THE RIGHT.*

1. The MOST common cause of death due to malignancy among females in the United States is from

   A. lung cancer
   C. skin cancer
   B. leukemia

   B. ovarian cancer
   D. colon and rectum cancer

   1._____

2. Medicare provides health coverage to people

   A. under 20 years of age
   B. who work of all ages
   C. greater than 65 years of age and end-stage renal dialysis patients
   D. under five years of age who require long-term hospitalization
   E. who need out-patient care only

   2._____

3. Insurance approaches to contain cost include managed care plans. A popular managed care approach has been

   A. Medicare
   B. Medicaid
   C. HMO's
   D. institutional reimbursement
   E. none of the above

   3._____

4. The occupational exposure that may lead to chronic interstitial pulmonary disease is

   A. silicosis
   C. asbestosis
   E. all of the above

   B. pneumoconiosis
   D. farmer's lung

   4._____

5. The principal mode of transmission of hepatitis A virus is

   A. blood transfusion
   C. fecal and oral route
   E. deer flies

   B. droplet nuclei
   D. mosquitoes

   5._____

6. The leading cause of death among diabetics after 20 years of diabetes is by

   A. infection
   B. cerebrovascular accident
   C. renal and cardiovascular disease
   D. diabetic ketoacidosis
   E. malignancy

   6._____

7. A breast-fed infant may require a supplementation of vitamin

   A. E   B. B_{12} C. K   D. D   E. A

   7._____

8. The MOST common organism associated with chronic active gastritis is

   A. salmonella
   C. campylobacter pylori
   E. rota virus

   B. shigella
   D. staphylococcus

   8._____

9. The large proportion of tuberculosis in older persons is due to
    A. recent exposure to tuberculosis
    B. reactivation of latent infection
    C. malnutrition
    D. immunosuppression
    E. substance abuse

9._____

10. The leading vector-borne disease in the United States is
    A. lyme disease
    B. Rocky Mountain spotted fever
    C. ehrlichiosis
    D. Q fever
    E. yellow fever

10._____

11. The malarial species causing the MOST fatal illness is
    A. P. vivax   B. P. falciparum
    C. P. malariae   D. P. cuale
    E. none of the above

11._____

Questions 12-16.

DIRECTIONS: Match the disease in Questions 12 through 16 with the associated animal in Column I.

12. Brucellosis   COLUMN I   12._____

13. Psittacosis   A. Bird   13._____
                                             B. Swine

14. Rabies   C. Rabbit   14._____
                                         D. Skunk

15. Tularemia   E. Cats   15._____

16. Toxoplasmosis   16._____

Questions 17-22.

DIRECTIONS: Match the trade in Questions 17 through 22 with the related occupational cancer in Column I.

17.   Pipefitters

18.   Rubber industry workers

19.   Radiologist

20.   Woodworkers

21.   Textile workers

22.   Chemists

COLUMN I

A.   Carcinoma of the bladder
B.   Mesothelioma
C.   Hodgkin's disease
D.   Leukemia
E.   Brain cancer
F.   Carcinoma of nasal cavity

17._____

18._____

19._____

20._____

21._____

22._____

Questions 23-25.

DIRECTIONS: Match the biostatistical description in Questions 23 through 25 with the related term in Column I.

23.   The presence of an event or characteristic at a single point in time

24.   Require a long period of observation

25.   The occurrence of an event or characteristic over a period of time

COLUMN I

A.   Incidence
B.   Prevalence
C.   Cohort study

23._____

24._____

25._____

_____

KEY (CORRECT ANSWERS)

1.	A		11.	B
2.	C		12.	B
3.	C		13.	A
4.	E		14.	D
5.	C		15.	C
6.	C		16.	E
7.	D		17.	B
8.	C		18.	A
9.	B		19.	D
10.	A		20.	C

21.   F·
22.   E
23.   B
24.   C
25.   A

_____

EXAMINATION SECTION
TEST 1

DIRECTIONS: Each question or incomplete statement is followed by several suggested answers or completions. Select the one that BEST answers the question or completes the statement. *PRINT THE LETTER OF THE CORRECT ANSWER IN THE SPACE AT THE RIGHT.*

Questions 1-4.

DIRECTIONS: Questions 1 through 4 are to be answered on the basis of the following information.

In a day care center of 30 children (20 females and 10 males), 7 boys develop hepatitis A over a 3-week period. During the next 8 weeks, an additional 2 boys and 5 girls develop the infection.

1. The attack rate of hepatitis A in this day care center is _____%.   1._____
    A. 20   B. 30   C. 40   D. 46.6   E. 54.5

2. The secondary attack rate of hepatitis A in this day care center is MOST NEARLY   2._____
    _____%.
    A. 20   B. 15   C. 23   D. 27   E. 10

3. The attack rate of hepatitis A for boys in this school is MOST NEARLY _____%.   3._____
    A. 16   B. 40   C. 50   D. 60   E. 64

4. The attack rate of hepatitis A for girls is MOST NEARLY _____%.   4._____
    A. 21   B. 24   C. 25   D. 27   E. 30

5. The epidemic curve suggests a common source outbreak with   5._____

    A. continuing common source outbreak
    B. fecal-oral transmission
    C. secondary airborne transmission
    D. secondary person-to-person transmission
    E. none of the above

6. The _____ rate is determined by the number of deaths caused by a specific disease   6._____
    divided by the number of cases of the disease.

    A. mortality   B. case fatality
    C. attack   D. cause specific death
    E. none of the above

7. Rate is the expression of the probability of occurrence of a particular event in a defined   7._____
    population during a specified period of time.
    The rate calculated for various segments of the population is known as the _____
    rate.

    A. specific   B. crude
    C. adjusted   D. variable
    E. none of the above

8. The sources of disease surveillance data include all of the following EXCEPT   8._____

    A.   individual case reports
    B.   emergency room visit records
    C.   hospital discharge summaries
    D.   death certificates
    E.   none of the above

9. All of the following are true about tularemia EXCEPT that it is   9._____

    A.   a zoonotic disease
    B.   more common during the summer months in the western states
    C.   more common in winter months in the eastern states
    D.   primarily transmitted by the bite of a spider
    E.   none of the above

10. Which of the following is NOT among the basic steps in an investigation of an epidemic?   10._____

    A.   Verification of diagnosis
    B.   Establishing the existence of an epidemic
    C.   Characterization of the distribution of cases
    D.   Formulating a conclusion
    E.   All of the above

11. The LAST step in conducting an epidemic investigation is to   11._____

    A.   develop an hypothesis
    B.   test the hypothesis
    C.   formulate a conclusion
    D.   institute control measures
    E.   establish the diagnosis of an epidemic

12. The patients who are infected with an agent but never develop clinical symptoms of the disease are known as _____ carriers.   12._____

    A.   incubatory   B.   subclinical   C.   chronic
    D.   convalescent   E.   clinical

13. All of the following are uses of epidemiology EXCEPT to   13._____

    A.   identify factors that cause disease
    B.   explain how and why diseases and epidemics occur
    C.   establish a clinical diagnosis of disease
    D.   determine a patient's prognosis
    E.   evaluate the effectiveness of health programs

14. The biological traits that determine the occurrence of a disease include all of the following EXCEPT   14._____

    A.   genetic characteristics   B.   diet
    C.   race   D.   ethnic origin
    E.   sex

15. The general factors of resistance in a human host include all of the following EXCEPT   15.____

    A. the immune system   B. intact skin
    C. diarrhea   D. normal bacterial flora
    E. gastric juices

16. All of the following are examples of direct contact transmission EXCEPT   16.____

    A. syphilis   B. herpes
    C. hepatitis B   D. sporotrichosis
    E. none of the above

17. The basic aims and specific goals of medical studies and clinical research do NOT include   17.____

    A. assessing health status or clinical characteristics
    B. eliminating all carriers of diseases
    C. determining and assessing treatment outcomes
    D. identifying and assessing risk factors
    E. all of the above

18. Incidence and prevalence studies usually concern all of the following EXCEPT   18.____

    A. the occurrence of disease
    B. a comparison of outcomes between different treatments
    C. adverse side effects of drugs
    D. the death rate for a certain disease
    E. none of the above

19. A case series report can address almost any clinical issue but it is MOST commonly used to describe   19.____

    A. clinical characteristics of a disease
    B. screening test results
    C. treatment outcomes
    D. an unexpected result or event
    E. none of the above

20. A comparison of chemotherapy to chemotherapy plus radiation for laryngeal carcinoma would be an appropriate topic for a(n)   20.____

    A. cohort study
    B. case control study
    C. clinical trial
    D. case series report
    E. incidence and prevalence study

21. The sum of all values in a series divided by the actual number of values in the series is known as the   21.____

    A. mode   B. median
    C. geometric mean   D. arithmetic mean
    E. none of the above

22. The MOST commonly occurring value in a series of values is the   22.____

    A. mode
    B. median
    C. geometric mean
    D. arithmetic mean
    E. none of the above

23. The ratio of the standard deviation of a series to the arithmetic mean of the series is   23.____
known as the

    A. range
    B. variance
    C. coefficient of variation
    D. standard deviation
    E. epidemic curve

24. The sum of squared deviations from the mean divided by the number of values in the   24.____
series minus 1 is called the

    A. range
    B. variance
    C. standard deviation
    D. coefficient of variation
    E. frequency polygon

25. The _____ is a tool for comparing categories of mutually exclusive discrete data.   25.____

    A. pie chart
    B. Venn diagram
    C. bar diagram
    D. histogram
    E. frequency polygon

KEY (CORRECT ANSWERS)

1.	D		11	D
2.	C		12.	B
3.	E		13.	D
4.	C		14.	B
5.	D		15.	A
6.	B		16.	E
7.	A		17.	B
8.	E		18.	B
9.	D		19.	A
10.	E		20.	C

21	D
22.	A
23.	C
24.	B
25.	C

TEST 2

DIRECTIONS: Each question or incomplete statement is followed by several suggested answers or completions. Select the one that BEST answers the question or completes the statement. *PRINT THE LETTER OF THE CORRECT ANSWER IN THE SPACE AT THE RIGHT.*

1. A _____ is a special form of the bar diagram used to represent categories of continuous and ordered data.   1._____

    A. pie chart
    B. histogram
    C. Venn diagram
    D. cumulative frequency graph
    E. frequency polygon

2. A medical student performs venipuncture on 1,000 randomly selected patients and is successful on the first attempt 700 times.
What is the probability that her next venipuncture will be successful on the first attempt?   2._____

    A. 7%   B. 14%   C. 50%   D. 70%   E. 80%

3. All of the following are true regarding the standard error of the mean of a sample EXCEPT that it   3._____

    A. is an estimate of the standard deviation of the population
    B. is based on a normal distribution
    C. increases as the sample size increases
    D. is used to determine confidence limits
    E. none of the above

4. All of the following are characteristics of a confidence interval EXCEPT that it   4._____

    A. is based on a critical ratio when the sample is large
    B. gives an indication of the likely magnitude of the true value
    C. gives an indication of the certainty of the point estimate
    D. becomes narrower as the sample size increases
    E. none of the above

5. Nonparametric tests can be used to compare two populations with which of the following conditions?   5._____

    A. Each population is unimodal
    B. Both populations have equal numbers
    C. Each population is independent
    D. Each population is distributed normally
    E. All of the above

6. All of the following vaccines are grown in embryonated chicken eggs EXCEPT   6._____

    A. yellow fever   B. measles   C. mumps
    D. rubella   E. influenza

7. Which of the following vaccines should NOT be given to individuals who live in house-   7.____
   holds with an immuno-compromised host?

   A. Yellow fever   B. Hepatitis B   C. Oral polio
   D. Influenza   E. Diphtheriae

8. A solution of antibodies derived from the serum of animals immunized with a specific   8.____
   antigen is a(n)

   A. immunoglobulin   B. antitoxin
   C. toxoid   D. vaccine
   E. none of the above

9. All of the following may be significant sequale of measles infection EXCEPT   9.____

   A. pneumonia
   B. encephalitis
   C. congenital birth defects
   D. . mental retardation
   E. death

10. All of the following statements about vaccination during pregnancy are true EXCEPT: 10.____

    A. Live attenuated viral vaccines should not be given to pregnant women
    B. Pregnant women at substantial risk of exposure may receive a live viral vaccine
    C. There is evidence that inactivated vaccines also pose risks to the fetus
    D. There is no evidence that immunoglobulins pose any risk to the fetus
    E. None of the above

11. None of the following conditions are reasons for delaying or discontinuing routine immu-   11.____
    nizations EXCEPT

    A. soreness, redness or swelling at the injection site in reaction to previous immuniza-
       tion
    B. a temperature of more than 105F in reaction to previous DTP vaccine
    C. mild diarrheal illness in an otherwise well child
    D. current antimicrobial therapy
    E. breastfeeding

12. Children and infants with any of the following disorders should not receive pertussis vac-   12.____
    cine EXCEPT those with

    A. uncontrolled epilepsy
    B. infantile spasms
    C. progressive encephalopathy
    D. developmental delay
    E. none of the above

13. Which of the following groups of patients should NOT receive pneumococcal polysaccha-   13.____
    ride vaccine?

    A. Elderly, age 65 or older
    B. Immunocompromised
    C. Children age 2 years or older with anatomic or functional asplenia

D. Children age 2 years or older with nephrotic syndrome or CSF leaks
E. Children under 2 years of age

14. All of the following are significant complications of sexually transmitted diseases in women EXCEPT

14.____

    A. pelvic inflammatory disease
    B. infertility
    C. teratogenicity
    D. cancer
    E. ectopic pregnancy

15. For primary prevention and maximal safety, a person should

15.____

    A. engage in a mutually monogamous relationship
    B. limit the number of sexual partners
    C. inspect and question new partners
    D. avoid sexual practices involving anal or fecal contact
    E. all of the above

16. All of the following are complications caused by untreated syphilis infection EXCEPT

16.____

    A. obesity   B. blindness
    C. psychosis   D. cardiovascular disease
    E. none of the above

17. All of the following statements are true regarding syphilis EXCEPT:

17.____

    A. The organism cannot enter through intact skin
    B. Everyone is susceptible
    C. There is no natural or acquired immunity
    D. No vaccine is available
    E. Reinfection is rare

18. Which of the following sexually transmitted diseases rank as the number one reported communicable disease in the United States?

18.____

    A. Syphilis   B. Gonorrhea   C. AIDS
    D. Chlamydia   E. Hepatitis B

19. Which of the following is believed to be the MOST common sexually transmitted bacterial pathogen in the United States?

19.____

    A. Treponema pallidum   B. Chlamydia trachomatis
    C. Nisseriae gonorrhea   D. E. coli
    E. Herpes zoster

20. All of the following are documented modes of transmission for human immunodeficiency virus EXCEPT _____ transmission.

20.____

    A. sexual   B. percutaneous exposure
    C. airborne   D. mother to child
    E. none of the above

21. In order to prevent HIV infection, which of the following groups should NOT donate blood?

    A.   Any man who has had sexual contact with another man since 1977
    B.   Present or past IV drug abusers
    C.   Individuals from Central Africa and Haiti
    D.   Sexual partners of any of the above groups
    E.   All of the above

21._____

22. Chlamydia trachomatis, the causative agent of chlamydia infection, has all of the following characteristics EXCEPT it

    A.   grows only intracellularly
    B.   contains both DNA and RNA
    C.   is a protozoa
    D.   divides by binary fission
    E.   has cell walls similar to gram-negative bacteriae

22._____

23. All of the following are true regarding the resultant effects of chlamydia trachomatis EXCEPT:

    A.   Approximately 50% cases of non-gonococcal urethritis in men
    B.   99% of cases of pelvic inflammatory disease
    C.   Mucopurulent cervicitis
    D.   Inclusion conjunctivitis in infants born to infected mothers
    E.   Acute epididymitis in men

23._____

24. All of the following statements are true regarding hepatitis A infection EXCEPT:

    A.   Approximately 70% of Americans are infected by the age of 20
    B.   Incidence appears to be declining
    C.   Infection is related to age and socioeconomic status
    D.   The incubation period is 15-50 days with an average of 28-30 days
    E.   Young children are more likely to have subclinical infections

24._____

25. The transmission of hepatitis A virus is facilitated by all of the following EXCEPT

    A.   poor personal hygiene
    B.   poor sanitation
    C.   drinking out of the same cup
    D.   eating uncooked or raw food
    E.   eating food contaminated by human hands after cooking

25._____

KEY (CORRECT ANSWERS)

1. B
2. D
3. C
4. E
5. E

6. D
7. C
8. B
9. C
10. C

11. B
12. D
13. E
14. C
15. E

16. A
17. E
18. B
19. B
20. C

21. E
22. C
23. B
24. A
25. C

EXAMINATION SECTION
TEST 1

DIRECTIONS: Each question or incomplete statement is followed by several suggested answers or completions. Select the one that BEST answers the question or completes the statement. *PRINT THE LETTER OF THE CORRECT ANSWER IN THE SPACE AT THE RIGHT.*

1. A PPD reaction of greater than or equal to 5 mm induration is considered positive in all of the following individuals EXCEPT

    A. persons with HIV infection
    B. IV drug abusers who are HIV antibody negative
    C. close recent contacts of an infectious tuberculosis case
    D. persons with a chest radiograph consistent with old, healed tuberculosis
    E. persons with HIV infection or with risk factors for HIV infection who have an unknown IV antibody status

1._____

2. All of the following are true about tuberculosis EXCEPT:

    A. The causative agent is M. tuberculosis var. hominis
    B. It is more likely to occur in older individuals (more than 45 years of age)
    C. It is more common in non-whites than in whites
    D. It is more common in men than in women
    E. About 90% of cases in the United States represent new infections

2._____

3. The groups that should benefit from preventive therapy for tuberculosis include all of the following EXCEPT

    A. individuals whose skin test has converted from negative to positive in the previous 2 years
    B. individuals with positive mantoux test and with HIV infection
    C. tuberculin-negative IV drug abusers
    D. tuberculin-positive individuals under 35 years of age
    E. individuals with immunosuppressive therapy who are tuberculin positive

3._____

4. INH prophylaxis should not be used in any of the following EXCEPT in

    A. the presence of clinical disease
    B. a pregnant woman who has recently converted to tuberculin positive
    C. patients with unstable hepatic function
    D. individuals who were previously adequately treated
    E. individuals with a previous adverse reaction to INH

4._____

5. What is the MOST common cause of bacterial meningitis in children under age 5?

    A. Streptococcus pneumoniae
    B. H. influenza
    C. N. meningitidis
    D. E. coli
    E. Staphylococcus aureus

5._____

6. All of the following are true about H. influenza infection EXCEPT: 6.____

    A. Peak incidence is from age 3 months to 2 years
    B. The mortality rate is about 5%
    C. Secondary spread to day care contacts under 4 years of age is rare
    D. About two-thirds of the cases occur in children under 15 months of age
    E. None of the above

7. All of the following statements are true about hemophilus influenza type B infection EXCEPT: 7.____

    A. Rifampin is the drug of choice for chemoprophylaxis
    B. Rifampin may be given to pregnant women
    C. The disease is more common in native and black Americans
    D. Humans are the reservoir of infections
    E. None of the above

8. All of the following statements are true about meningococcal meningitis EXCEPT: 8.____

    A. It is the second most common cause of bacterial meningitis in the United States
    B. The peak incidence is around age 6-12 months
    C. Most cases occur in late winter and early spring
    D. The portal of entry is not the nasopharynx
    E. It is more likely to occur in newly aggregated young adults who are living in institutions and barracks

9. Antimicrobial chemoprophylaxis is the chief preventive measure in sporadic cases of meningococcal meningitis and should be offered to   9.____

    A. household contacts
    B. day care center contacts
    C. medical personnel who resuscitated, intubated or suctioned the patient before antibiotics were instituted
    D. all patients who were treated for meningococcal disease before discharge from the hospital
    E. all of the above

10. What is the MOST common cause of bacterial meningitis in children under 5 years of age?   10.____

    A. Streptococcus pneumoniae
    B. Nisseriae meningitidis
    C. Listeria monocytogenes
    D. Group B streptococcus
    E. Hemophilus influenza type B

11. All of the following are true about coronary heart disease EXCEPT: 11.____

    A. It is the leading cause of death in the United States
    B. About 4.6 million Americans have coronary heart disease
    C. It is most common in white men
    D. Women have a greater risk of myocardial infarction and sudden death
    E. Women have a greater risk of angina pectoris

12. According to the National Cholesterol Education Panel, which of the following is NOT a major risk factor for coronary artery disease?   12._____

    A. Women 55 years and older
    B. Hypertension
    C. Individuals with diabetes mellitus
    D. High density lipoprotein (HDL) less than 35 mg/dl
    E. Obesity

13. The number one cause of cancer death in the United States is _____ cancer.   13._____

    A. lung   B. breast   C. colorectal
    D. cervical   E. prostatic

14. The MOST common cancer in American men is _____ cancer.   14._____

    A. lung   B. breast   C. prostate
    D. colon   E. esophageal

15. All of the following are risk factors for women to develop breast cancer EXCEPT   15._____

    A. exposure to ionizing radiation
    B. becoming pregnant for the first time after age 30
    C. mother and sisters having breast cancer
    D. high socioeconomic status
    E. late menarchae

16. Cervical cancer is one of the leading causes of death among women.
Of the following, which is NOT a risk factor for developing cervical cancer?   16._____

    A. Multiple sexual partners
    B. First coitus before age 20
    C. Low socioeconomic status
    D. Oral contraceptive use
    E. Partners of uncircumcised men

17. Population subgroups at INCREASED risk of developing anemia include   17._____

    A. women   B. elderly men
    C. children   D. blacks
    E. all of the above

18. Uncontrolled hypertensive disease increases the risk of developing all of the following disorders EXCEPT   18._____

    A. coronary heart disease   B. diabetes mellitus
    C. renal disease   D. cerebrovascular disease
    E. none of the above

19. All of the following statements are true regarding chronic obstructive pulmonary disease (COPD) EXCEPT: 19._____

    A. Men are at higher risk than women
    B. An estimated 16 million Americans have chronic bronchitis, asthma or emphysema
    C. The risk is related to the duration of smoking only

D. The risk is related to the number of cigarettes smoked daily and to the duration of smoking
E. Offspring of affected individuals are at higher risk

20. Which of the following statements is TRUE regarding diabetes in the United States?   20._____

   A. It accounts for 5% of all deaths.
   B. Its prevalence is estimated at 15%.
   C. 80% of all diabetics have the non-insulin dependent type.
   D. It is the leading cause of blindness.
   E. Men are at greater risk than women.

21. People with increased risk for suicide include all of the following EXCEPT   21._____

   A. drug users   B. married individuals
   C. teenagers   D. chronically depressed
   E. homosexuals

22. Conditions associated with an increased risk for suicide include all of the following EXCEPT   22._____

   A. unemployed
   B. seriously physically ill or handicapped
   C. chronically mentally ill
   D. substance abusers
   E. none of the above

23. The leading cause of death among black men aged 15-24 years is   23._____

   A. automobile accidents   B. homicide
   C. cancer   D. drug abuse
   E. AIDS

24. All of the following are true regarding pernicious anemia EXCEPT: 24._____

   A. It primarily affects individuals over the age of 30
   B. The incidence increases with age
   C. It is more common in Asians and blacks
   D. It is caused by a vitamin B_{12} deficiency
   E. None of the above

25. Which of the following groups of individuals have a high risk of injuries?   25._____

   A. Factory workers
   B. Alcoholics
   C. Individuals with osteoporosis
   D. Homeless
   E. All of the above

KEY (CORRECT ANSWERS)

1.	B		11.	D
2.	E		12.	D
3.	C		13.	A
4.	B		14.	C
5.	B		15.	E
6.	C		16.	C
7.	B		17.	E
8.	D		18.	B
9.	E		19.	C
10.	E		20.	D

21.	B
22.	E
23.	B
24.	C
25.	E

TEST 2

DIRECTIONS: Each question or incomplete statement is followed by several suggested answers or completions. Select the one that BEST answers the question or completes the statement. *PRINT THE LETTER OF THE CORRECT ANSWER IN THE SPACE AT THE RIGHT.*

1. Which of the following factors does NOT increase a woman's risk of an ectopic pregnancy?   1.____

   A. Progestin exposure
   B. Pelvic inflammatory disease
   C. Smoking
   D. Use of alcohol
   E. Infertility

2. Breastfeeding usually enhances all of the following EXCEPT   2.____

   A. bonding between mother and infant
   B. infant nutrition
   C. immune defenses
   D. antibody response against HIV virus
   E. return of uterus to prepregnant size

3. Which of the following is NOT a leading cause of maternal mortality in the United States?   3.____

   A. Hypertensive disease of pregnancy
   B. Cardiovascular accidents
   C. Miscarriage
   D. Anesthesia complications
   E. All of the above

4. A well-woman prenatal visit should include all of the following EXCEPT a(n)   4.____

   A. weight check
   B. blood pressure check
   C. electronic fetal monitoring
   D. pap smear
   E. urine analysis

5. All of the following substances or conditions are harmful to the fetus during gestation EXCEPT   5.____

   A. tetracycline   B. alcohol   C. herpes
   D. rubella   E. thalidomide

6. The use of an intrauterine device (IUD) has been associated with increased risk of   6.____

   A. ectopic pregnancy
   B. pelvic inflammatory disease
   C. infertility
   D. infections
   E. all of the above

7. The number of deaths among infants less than 28 days old per 1,000 live births is called   7._____
    the _____ mortality rate.

    A. neonatal   B. post-neonatal
    C. fetal   D. perinatal
    E. none of the above

8. All of the following are causes of postneonatal mortality EXCEPT   8._____

    A. lower respiratory tract infections
    B. intrauterine growth retardation
    C. congenital anomalies
    D. sudden infant death syndrome
    E. injuries, e.g., motor vehicle accidents

9. All of the following are important factors in the identification of high risk parents and in the   9._____
    management and prevention of infant health problems EXCEPT

    A. intrauterine infections
    B. pre-existing maternal illnesses
    C. paternal age
    D. maternal history of reproductive problems
    E. family history of hereditary disease

10. Screening for which of the following conditions has been proven to be cost effective?   10._____

    A. Phenylketonuria   B. Congenital hypothyroidism
    C. Lead poisoning   D. Tuberculosis
    E. All of the above

11. Children _____ are more likely to receive inadequate well-child care.   11._____

    A. with chronic health problems
    B. on medicaid
    C. of mothers who started receiving prenatal care late in the second or third trimester
    D. of parents whose jobs do not provide health insurance
    E. all of the above

12. Injuries are classified by the intent or purposefulness of occurrence.   12._____
    All of the following are classified as intentional injuries EXCEPT

    A. child abuse   B. motor vehicle mishaps
    C. sexual assault   D. domestic violence
    E. abuse of the elderly

13. Schizophrenia is a disorder, or group of disorders, with a variety of symptoms that   13._____
    include

    A. delusions   B. hallucinations
    C. agitation   D. apathy
    E. all of the above

14. All of the following are true about the incidence and prevalence of bipolar disorder   14._____
    EXCEPT:

A. Approximately 4-5% of the population is at risk
B. More women are admitted to the hospital with the diagnosis of bipolar disorder than men
C. The manic form occurs primarily in younger individuals
D. Bipolar patients are more likely to be unmarried
E. The depressive form occurs primarily in older individuals

15. In schizophrenia, there is an increased risk for all of the following EXCEPT   15._____

A. malabsorption syndrome
B. arteriosclerotic heart disease
C. hypothyroidism
D. cancer
E. none of the above

16. A 6-month-old Jewish infant has a history of seizures, progressive blindness, deafness,   16._____
and paralysis with an exaggerated startle response to sound.
The MOST likely diagnosis is

A. phenylketonuria   B. Gaucher's disease
C. Tay Sachs disease   D. homocystinuria
E. maple syrup disease

17. The MOST common inborn error of amino acid metabolism results in   17._____

A. phenylketonuria   B. maple syrup disease
C. homocystinuria   D. albinism
E. Gaucher's disease

18. The MOST common lysosomal storage disease is   18._____

A. Niemann-Pick disease   B. Gaucher's disease
C. Tay Sachs disease   D. homocystinuria
E. none of the above

19. All of the following are true about spina bifida EXCEPT: 19._____

A. The most common type is spina bifida occulta
B. The least severe form is myelocoele
C. Encephalocoele is the rarest type
D. The most common site affected is lower back
E. The familial risk of recurrence is approximately 5%

Questions 20-25.

DIRECTIONS: For each metal listed in Questions 20 through 25, select the condition in the
column below that is MOST likely to result from chronic exposure to it.

20. Lead   A. Osteomalacia-like disease   20._____
21. Arsenic   B. Granulomas of skin and lungs   21._____
22. Cadmium   C. Abnormal sperms   22._____
23. Mercury   D. Nasal septal ulceration   23._____
24. Beryllium   E. Visual field abnormalities   24._____
25. Zinc   F. Metal fume fever   25._____

KEY (CORRECT ANSWERS)

1.	D	11.	E
2.	D	12.	B
3.	C	13.	E
4.	C	14.	D
5.	C	15.	D
6.	E	16.	C
7.	A	17.	A
8.	B	18.	C
9.	C	19.	B
10.	E	20.	C

21.	D
22.	A
23.	E
24.	B
25.	F

EXAMINATION SECTION
TEST 1

DIRECTIONS: Each question or incomplete statement is followed by several suggested answers or completions. Select the one that BEST answers the question or completes the statement. *PRINT THE LETTER OF THE CORRECT ANSWER IN THE SPACE AT THE RIGHT.*

1. The MAJOR determinant of a material's hazard potential is

    A.   where it enters the body
    B.   how it is used
    C.   how it reacts with other substances
    D.   its toxicity
    E.   level of exposure

1._____

2. Injection is an imperfect way of getting toxic materials into the body to gain knowledge of potential industrial hazards because

    A.   the effects vary with the route of administration
    B.   few workers are exposed by injection
    C.   no needle is totally nontoxic
    D.   it is a costly procedure
    E.   the protective mechanisms of the body are bypassed

2._____

3. A single large dose of a toxic substance may be expected to produce a GREATER response than the same total dose administered over a long period of time because

    A.   there is no cumulative effect associated with toxic substances
    B.   small doses are easily absorbed into the bloodstream
    C.   there is no target organ when the toxic substances produce no measurable effect
    D.   small doses are detoxified before detrimental action occurs
    E.   there is no difference in response

3._____

4. Which of the following *correctly* characterizes an acute effect?

    A.   Frequent and recurring
    B.   Sudden and severe
    C.   Long-term and low level
    D.   Lethal
    E.   Insidious and accumulative

4._____

5. The difference between smokers and non-smokers is especially acute in studies involving exposure to

    A.   hydrogen cyanide   B.   carbon dioxide
    C.   methane   D.   hydrogen sulfide
    E.   carbon monoxide

5._____

6. Which of the following defines MOST precisely the time relationship and the magnitude of the risk for exposure to substances?

    A.   Retrospective studies of epidemiological data
    B.   Descriptive studies of epidemiological data

6._____

C. Prospective studies of epidemiological data
D. Animal experimentation
E. Chemical analogy

7. The advantages of biological monitoring over air sampling are that   7._____
    I.   substances absorbed through the skin and gastrointestinal tract are accounted for
    II. individual TLVs can be established
    III. the effects of stress are reflected in the analytical results
    IV. variations between individual responses within a group can be charted
    V. the total exposure on and off the job can be accounted for

The CORRECT answer is:

A. I, II, III, IV   B. I, II, IV
C. I, III, IV   D. I, III, V
E. none of the above

8. The toxicity of any chemical is dependent upon   8._____

A. its effect on the body
B. the level it can be tolerated without effect
C. physiological state
D. the degree of exposure
E. environmental conditions

9. Which region of skin has the HIGHEST penetration potential?   9._____

A. Back of the hand   B. Forehead
C. Abdomen   D. Forearm
E. Palm of the hand

10. The LOWEST concentration that produces death in 100% of the exposed animals is   10._____
expressed as

A. LD   B. LD_{50} C. LD_0 D. LD_{001} E. LD_{100}

11. An effect is considered local when   11._____

A. the route of entry is by skin absorption
B. only the target organ is affected
C. exposure does not change normal functioning
D. the substance harms only that part of the body with which it comes in contact
E. the substance has a systemic effect

12. Workers exposed to benzidine are MORE likely to get   12._____

A. lung cancer   B. leukemia
C. bone cancer   D. bladder cancer
E. intestinal cancer

13. How do most physical stresses relate to the toxic response of a substance?   13._____

A. Only ultraviolet and ionizing radiation show increases
B. Most have no effect
C. Most decrease the effect

D. Most increase the effect

E. There is no relationship between toxicity and physical stress

14. A lead-in-air sampling is NOT a good indicator to hazardous exposure because   14.____
    I. some lead particles are too large to get into the alveoli of the lung
    II. some lead ore is extremely insoluable
    III. inorganic lead is not absorbed
    IV. intake of lead is mostly by ingestion
    V. lead particles' settling rate is rapid

    The CORRECT answer is:

    A. I, II   B. I, II, III
    C. I, IV, V   D. II, III, IV
    E. II, IV, V

15. Which of the following statements is TRUE?   15.____

    A. Materials of the same toxicity represent equal hazards.
    B. Toxicity determines the degree of hazard.
    C. The degree of hazard determines toxicity.
    D. Toxicity is a factor in determining the degree of hazard.
    E. Materials that have the same degree of hazard have the same toxicity.

16. The MAIN determinant of whether or not a material will be absorbed through the skin is   16.____
    the

    A. pH of the skin
    B. temperature
    C. physiochemical properties of the material
    D. toxicity of the material
    E. sensitization of the skin

17. The MOST important route of entry for industrial exposure to chemicals is by   17.____

    A. inhalation   B. skin absorption
    C. injection   D. ingestion
    E. infection

18. Lethal dose is determined from the exposure to a substance by any route other than   18.____

    A. ingestion   B. inhalation
    C. infection   D. injection
    E. skin absorption

19. What does LD_{50} express about the effects of the concentration on the animals tested?   19.____

    A. Half the exposed animals died.
    B. Half the exposed animals lived.
    C. There was no effect on half the exposed animals.
    D. Half the exposed animals became ill or died.
    E. 500 per million are expected to die.

20. Which of the following BEST expresses the meaning of chronic poisoning?   20.____

    A. Some level of material will be continuously present in the tissues.
    B. Exposure involves low concentrations.

C. Rapid absorption of the material follows exposure.
D. There is little or no reaction to the exposure.
E. Reaction to exposure is rarely cumulative.

21. According to their physiological action, aliphatic alcohols, aliphatic ketones and hydrocarbons are considered

21.____

    A. cardiac sensitizers   B. asphyxiants
    C. anesthetics   D. neurotoxic agents
    E. irritants

22. Which part of the body is particularly sensitive to organometallic compounds?

22.____

    A. Eyes   B. Skin
    C. Liver   D. Kidneys
    E. Central nervous system

23. The substances that are designated with the letter "C" (Ceiling value) are

23.____

    A. carcinogens   B. narcotics
    C. asphyxiants   D. irritants
    E. anesthetics

24. The LEAST useful toxicological data are those based upon

24.____

    A. short-term oral intake by experimental animals
    B. short-term injecting of experimental animals
    C. long-term inhalation tests of experimental animals
    D. human experience
    E. epidemiological studies

25. It is difficult to set standard values by the use of gas chromatography or infrared analysis of breath samples because

25.____

    A. identification of the substance after a short period of time is near impossible
    B. most inhaled gases and vapors are not cleared through the respiratory system
    C. the magnitude of exposure cannot be determined
    D. the test offers no indication of probable blood levels
    E. there is considerable individual variation of breath decay rate

KEY (CORRECT ANSWERS)

1.	B	11.	D
2.	E	12.	D
3.	D	13.	D
4.	B	14.	B
5.	E	15.	D
6.	C	16.	C
7.	D	17.	A
8.	D	18.	B
9.	B	19.	A
10.	E	20.	A

21.	C
22.	E
23.	D
24.	A
25.	E

TEST 2

DIRECTIONS: Each question or incomplete statement is followed by several suggested answers or completions. Select the one that BEST answers the question or completes the statement. *PRINT THE LETTER OF THE CORRECT ANSWER IN THE SPACE AT THE RIGHT.*

1. A very good index of the probable damage resulting from lead exposure is obtained by

    A. urine samples
    B. breath analysis
    C. air sampling
    D. hair samples
    E. blood samples

1._____

2. The concept of synergism MUST be understood in evaluating oncogenic agents because

    A. synergism describes the body's ability to resist mutation
    B. synergistic substances act like antibodies
    C. synergism removes mutagens from the environment
    D. only some forms of toxins may be considered synergistic
    E. synergistic effects of unknown contaminants alter the hazard of carcinogen substances

2._____

3. The MAJOR cause of environmental cancer are tobacco smoke and

    A. industry
    B. diet
    C. polluted air
    D. polluted water
    E. chemical exposure

3._____

4. Which of the following irritants affect the upper respiratory tract?
    I. Formaldehyde
    II. Ammonia
    III. Sulfur dioxide
    IV. Nitrogen dioxide
    V. Phosgene
    The CORRECT answer is:

    A. I, II, III
    B. I, II, V
    C. II, III, IV
    D. II, IV, V
    E. III, IV

4._____

5. The margin of safety is slight when the dose-response curve is

    A. nearly horizontal
    B. bell-shaped
    C. nearly vertical
    D. gradually slanted vertically
    E. gradually slanted horizontally

5._____

6. The dose of a dose-response relationship involves BOTH

    A. concentration and duration of exposure
    B. concentration and unit of body weight
    C. quantity and unit of body weight
    D. concentration and condition
    E. toxicity and physical characteristics

6._____

7. Ingested materials may be absorbed into the blood via the

    A. respiratory tract   B. liver
    C. intestines   D. kidneys
    E. pleural cavity

7._____

8. Breath analysis is MOST useful for

    A. methyl bromide   B. tellurium
    C. chlorohydrocarbons   D. nickel carbonyl
    E. benzene

8._____

9. Analysis of urine samples should be useful for

    A. lead   B. arsenic
    C. carbon monoxide   D. chlorohydrocarbons
    E. cadium dust

9._____

10. A teratogen is different from a mutagen in that

    A. only a presently developing fetus is affected
    B. the effect is hereditary
    C. smokers are more at risk than non-smokers
    D. the mutation may not appear for several generations
    E. both the pregnant woman and her fetus is affected

10._____

11. Simple asphyxiants

    A. keep the oxygen level far below what it should be
    B. prevent the uptake of oxygen by the blood
    C. interfere with the transporting of oxygen from the lungs to the tissues
    D. prevent normal oxygenation of tissues
    E. do not result in death

11._____

12. What designation is used to express the lethal effect of airborne materials?

    A. LA   B. LI   C. LR   D. LD   E. LC

12._____

13. The severity of the action of the toxic agent is a function of

    A. the route of entry
    B. how the material gains entry into the bloodstream
    C. the duration of exposure
    D. the concentration of the substance in the target organ
    E. physiological function

13._____

14. Ingested toxic materials that are absorbed into the bloodstream may be detoxified by the

    A. intestines   B. kidneys
    C. spleen   D. gall bladder
    E. liver

14._____

15. Adverse reactions to substances are dependent upon all the following EXCEPT the

    A. properties of the chemical
    B. dose
    C. route of entry

15._____

D. susceptibility of the exposed individual
E. environment

16. Threshold limit values are intended for use
    I. as a relative index of hazard
    II. in the evaluation of community air pollution nuisances
    III. in estimating the toxic potential of continuous, uninterrupted exposures
    IV. as proof or disproof of work-related physical conditions
    V. by countries whose working conditions are the same as those in the U.S.
The CORRECT answer is:

A. I, II, IV
C. II, III, IV, V
E. all of the above

B. I, IV, V
D. IV, V

16.____

17. The presence of Hippuric acid in the urine indicates exposure to

A. methyl alcohol
C. aniline
E. benzene

B. phenol
D. toluene

17.____

18. The problem of time lag between exposure and effect is MOST severe for

A. carcinogens
C. mutagens
E. neurotoxic agents

B. terztogens
D. oncogens

18.____

19. Which of the following is TRUE of the Toxic Substances List?

A. All substances listed must be avoided.
B. Absence of a substance from the list indicates lack of toxicity.
C. All listed substances have a documented potential of being hazardous if misused.
D. All listed substances must be avoided by pregnant females and used with care by females of child-bearing age.
E. All substances listed are suspected or proven hazards.

19.____

20. Which of the following are *correctly* identified?
    I. Carbon dioxide - chemical asphyxiant
    II. Methane - simple asphyxiant
    III. Hydrogen sulfide - simple asphyxiant
    IV. Hydrogen cyanide - chemical asphyxiant
    V. Carbon monoxide - simple asphyxiant
The CORRECT answer is:

A. I, II, III
C. II, IV, V
E. IV, V

B. II, IV
D. III, IV, V

20.____

21. Which of the following is NOT critical to the LD value?

A. Species of the experimental animal
B. Route of administration of the compound
C. Vehicle used to dissolve or suspend the material
D. Length of time the exposure was maintained
E. Time period over which the animals were observed

21.____

22. Lethal concentration data is *only* meaningful when it includes the

    I.   species of experimental animal
    II.   route of administration of the compound
    III. vehicle used to dissolve or suspend the material
    IV. length of time the exposure was maintained
    V.   length of time observation was carried out after exposure

The CORRECT answer is:

22._____

A. I, II, III, V
C. I, IV, V
E. all of the above

B. I, II, V
D. II, IV, V

23. The relationship between the dose of the chemical and the response that is produced in a biological system defines the

23._____

A. severity of the action of the toxic agent
B. toxic effect
C. toxic potency of a chemical
D. degree of hazard
E. threshold of effect

24. Oral toxicity is *generally* LOWER than inhalation toxicity for the same material because

24._____

A. absorption into the blood from the intestines is poor
B. there is a constant flow of mucous
C. detoxification takes place in the stomach
D. excretion takes place through the kidney and urinary tract
E. food and liquid mixed with a toxic substance provides an opportunity to form a more soluble substance

25. Which of the following are TRUE of irritation?

25._____

    I.   The degree of local irritation is related to the systemic toxicities of the substance.
    II.   The viscosity of an irritant liquid can determine the type of injury.
    III. The solubility of an irritant gas can influence the part of the respiratory tract affected.
    IV. Chemical irritants produce an immediate reaction.
    V.   Short-term exposures are usually reversible.

The CORRECT answer is:

A. I, II, III
C. II, III
E. all of the above

B. I, III, V
D. II, III, V

KEY (CORRECT ANSWERS)

1.	E		11.	A
2.	E		12.	E
3.	B		13.	D
4.	A		14.	E
5.	C		15.	E
6.	A		16.	D
7.	C		17.	D
8.	C		18.	C
9.	B		19.	C
10.	A		20.	B

21.	D
22.	C
23.	C
24.	A
25.	D

TEST 3

DIRECTIONS: Each question or incomplete statement is followed by several suggested answers or completions. Select the one that BEST answers the question or completes the statement. *PRINT THE LETTER OF THE CORRECT ANSWER IN THE SPACE AT THE RIGHT.*

1. The *usual* method of providing protection when air contaminants may injure the health of workers is

    A. substitution with a less harmful material
    B. change of process
    C. personal protective devices
    D. enclosure of the worker
    E. ventilation

1.____

2. An example of a "change of a process" to minimize worker exposure is

    A. shot blasting instead of sand blasting
    B. use of freon instead of methyl bromide as a refrigerant
    C. removing beryllium phosphors from formulations for fluorescent lamps
    D. using pelletized forms of materials
    E. use of airless paint spraying techniques

2.____

3. The MAJOR disadvantages of general ventilation are
    I. a large volume of dilution air is needed
    II. ventilation may be inefficient
    III. high velocities of air are needed
    IV. hood selection is crucial to proper functioning
    V. employee exposures are difficult to control
The CORRECT answer is:

    A. I, II, V   B. I, III, V
    C. II, III, IV   D. III, V
    E. all of the above

3.____

4. The hazard that *usually* requires the MOST stringent medical controls is

    A. airborne bacteria   B. hydrocarbon vapors
    C. ultrasonic radiation   D. radioactive dusts
    E. radar emissions

4.____

5. The interaction between the health professional and the engineer is the MOST beneficial

    A. before operations begin
    B. when there is evidence of a *hazard*
    C. when administrative control methods are inadequate
    D. when the plant is being designed
    E. whenever a complaint is registered

5.____

6. Operations that generate contaminants in large quantities are BEST controlled by

    A. local exhaust ventilation
    B. good housekeeping

6.____

C. isolation
D. medical controls
E. personal protective devices

7. The personal protective equipment that should *only* be used for emergency or short-term protection is   7.____

     A. protective creams
     B. protective clothing
     C. respirators
     D. hearing protection
     E. eye and face protectors

8. The extent of the medical controls is determined by   8.____

     A. engineering guidelines
     B. the hazards and seriousness of the risks involved
     C. symptoms of exposure
     D. the manner in which the hazard is controlled
     E. the absorption capabilities of the toxic materials

9. The hand cleanser that provides a feeling of removing soils because of stimulation of the nerve endings in the skin by the abrasives present is   9.____

     A. liquid cleaners
     B. soap cakes
     C. cream soaps
     D. powdered soaps
     E. waterless hand cleaners

10. Significant reductions in airborne dust concentrations in rock drilling operations have been achieved by   10.____

     A. use of water
     B. ventilation
     C. use of personal protective devices
     D. good housekeeping
     E. administrative exposure controls

11. Problems NOT anticipated during the design stage are MOST likely to manifest themselves   11.____

     A. when the unit or process is put into operation
     B. during loading operations
     C. when on-site reviews are made
     D. when the sampling system is implemented
     E. when an actual exposure occurs

12. Medical controls are so important because   12.____

     A. they can serve as verification of the engineering controls
     B. dose-response relationships can be deduced
     C. they detect any deleterious effects of work

D. they identify workers unduly susceptible to toxic agents
E. all of the above

13. An example of an administrative method for controlling environmental factors or stresses is   13.____

   A. adjusting work schedules
   B. educating employees
   C. providing protective devices
   D. proper disposal of wastes
   E. medical surveillance program

14. The LEAST desirable method for controlling a contaminant is   14.____

   A. isolation
   B. changing the process
   C. substitution
   D. local exhaust ventilation
   E. enclosure

15. All of the following are good substitute solvents EXCEPT   15.____

   A. methyl chloroform
   B. aliphatic petroleum hydrocarbon
   C. carbon tetrachloride
   D. dichloromethane
   E. fluorochlorohydrocarbon

16. Shielding is one of the better control methods used to reduce or eliminate exposures to   16.____

   A. noise
   B. air contaminants
   C. heat and ionizing radiation
   D. ultraviolet and infrared radiations
   E. biological hazards

17. The proper design of exhaust ventilation depends on the   17.____
   I. temperature of the process
   II. physical state of the contaminant
   III. manner in which the contaminant is generated
   IV. velocity in which it is released
   V. contaminant's toxicity
The CORRECT answer is:

   A. I, II, IV   B. II, III, V
   C. III, IV, V   D. IV, V
   E. all of the above

18. The LEAST expensive and MOST positive method of controlling occupational health hazards is   18.____

   A. isolation or enclosure of a process
   B. substitution of a less hazardous material
   C. administrative exposure controls

D. change of process
E. dilution ventilation

19. Which of the following process changes will MINIMIZE the presence of airborne contam-   19.____
inants?

    I. Riveting replacing arc-welding
    II. Compressed air spraying replacing airless paint spraying
    III. Vapor degreasing in tanks (with ventilation) replacing hand-washing of parts in open containers
    IV. Low-speed oscillating sanders replacing small, rotary high-speed sanders
    V. Dipping replacing spray painting

The CORRECT answer is:

A. I, II, III   B. I, III, V
C. II, III, V   D. III, IV, V
E. IV, V

20. The BEST way to protect workers is   20.____

A. to conduct operations in entirely closed systems
B. continuous area monitoring
C. personal monitoring devices
D. local and area ventilation systems
E. to isolate operations

21. The degree to which any possibility of leakage is engineered or designed out of a system   21.____
is determined by

A. periodic check-ups
B. level of maintenance
C. anticipating potential leaks
D. training and education of workers
E. type of operation

22. Ventilation systems are MOST useful when   22.____

A. few workers are involved
B. the process has been isolated
C. personal protection devices are in use
D. the potential risk for exposure is low
E. very toxic materials must be processed

23. The effectiveness of wet methods for dust control depend chiefly on   23.____

A. type of dust involved
B. the area of concentration
C. the dust producing operation
D. the toxicity of the dust
E. proper wetting of the dust

24. General ventilation should NOT be used when   24.____

A. air contaminants are released at a uniform rate
B. contaminants are highly toxic

C. there is sufficient distance between the worker and the source of the contaminant
D. the contaminant can be discharged into the community environment
E. natural convection is present

25. The MOST serious drawback to personal protective devices is that   25._____

A. they put safety in the hands of the workers
B. they do nothing to reduce or eliminate the hazard
C. they only offer emergency or short-term protection
D. it is costly to fit individual workers
E. their effectivenss is the result of short-term test results

———————

KEY (CORRECT ANSWERS)

1.	E		11.	A
2.	E		12.	E
3.	A		13.	A
4.	D		14.	D
5.	D		15.	C
6.	C		16.	C
7.	C		17.	E
8.	B		18.	B
9.	D		19.	D
10.	A		20.	A

21.	C
22.	B
23.	E
24.	B
25.	B

———————

EXAMINATION SECTION
TEST 1

DIRECTIONS: Each question or incomplete statement is followed by several suggested answers or completions. Select the one that BEST answers the question or completes the statement. *PRINT THE LETTER OF THE CORRECT ANSWER IN THE SPACE AT THE RIGHT.*

1. The responsibility that the worker make proper use of the protective equipment provided by management that is designed to reduce noise exposure lies with the   1.____

    A. management   B. safety professional
    C. medical staff   D. industrial hygienist
    E. worker

2. Signs of heat exhaustion include   2.____
        I. weak pulse
       II. warm, dry skin
     III. dizziness
     IV. mildly reduced temperature
      V. pallor

The CORRECT answer is:

    A. I, II, III   B. I, II, IV   C. I, II, V   D. I, III, V
    E. all of the above

3. The amount of energy a particular kind of radioactive material possesses is defined in terms of   3.____

    A. Hz   B. atomic number   C. half life   D. mass number
    E. MeV

4. The finger that possesses an additional extensor muscle and is not well adapted for repetitive flexing action is the   4.____

    A. thumb   B. index finger
    C. middle finger   D. ring finger
    E. little finger

5. Particles of dust considered to be of respirable size are less than _____ micrometer.   5.____

    A. 3   B. 5   C. 7   D. 10   E. 15

6. The LEAST desirable training background for an industrial hygienist would be in   6.____

    A. engineering   B. physics
    C. biology   D. chemistry
    E. psychology

7. The responsibility of the safety professional is to   7.____

    A. determine the general healthfulness of the environment
    B. determine employee response to the work environment
    C. correlate employee complaints with potential hazard areas
    D. select workers for job assignments
    E. see that control measures are applied and followed

8. The inhalation of dusts or fumes is a _____ hazard.   8._____

    A. chemical   B. physical
    C. biological   D. ergonomic
    E. environmental

9. The MAJORITY of environmental health hazards arise from   9._____

    A. inhaling chemical agents
    B. exposure to radiation
    C. bacterial contamination of food and objects
    D. improperly designed tools and work areas
    E. lack of personal cleanliness

10. Chemical agents which represent the greatest danger to health may enter the body by   10._____
inhalation in all the following forms EXCEPT

    A. vapors   B. gases
    C. dust   D. solids
    E. mists

11. Concentrations of inert gases in the environment *might* result in   11._____

    A. corneal damage
    B. damage to reproductive tissue
    C. chemical asphyxia
    D. hypertension
    E. inert gas poisoning

12. By definition, the flashpoint for a flammable liquid must be   12._____

    A. 451° F.   B. 100° C.
    C. 32° C.   D. 100° F.
    E. 212° F.

13. The device that is used to measure radiant heat is called a(n)   13._____

    A. globe thermometer   B. anemometer
    C. hygromometer   D. kelvin thermometer
    E. bathe thermograph

14. The type of radiation that is MOST easily screened and is NOT a serious health hazard is   14._____
_____ particles.

    A. alpha   B. beta
    C. neutron   D. x-ray
    E. gamma

15. The field of study dealing with the physiological and psychological stresses of the work   15._____
place is

    A. biomechanics   B. industrial physiology
    C. ergonomics   D. stressology
    E. transactional analysis

16. The effects of exposure to a substance are NOT dependent upon

    A. temperature   B. age
    C. site of absorption   D. diet
    E. general state of health

16.＿＿＿

17. Which of the following compounds may penetrate deeply into the lungs but, due to their insolubility in body fluids, cause little or no throat irritation?

    I. Formaldehyde
    II. Sulfuric acid
    III. Nitrogen dioxide
    IV. Ozone
    V. Hydrochloric acid

The CORRECT answer is:

    A. I, II, IV   B. I, III, V
    C. II, III, IV   D. II, V
    E. III, IV

17.＿＿＿

18. Which of the following is NOT an acceptable method for controlling harmful environmental factors or stresses?

    A. Substitution of less harmful material for one that is hazardous
    B. Local exhaust at the point of generation and dispersion
    C. Personal protective devices
    D. Medical programs to detect intake of toxic materials
    E. Strict screening of employees during the hiring procedure

18.＿＿＿

19. The MOST elementary factor of environmental control is control of

    A. the thermal environment
    B. the noise level
    C. dangerous materials
    D. radiation
    E. ergonomic stress

19.＿＿＿

20. The moisture content of the air is *generally* measured with a(n)

    A. anemometer   B. psychrometer
    C. barometer   D. hygromometer
    E. kelvin thermometer

20.＿＿＿

21. A toxic gas that directly affects lung tissue is

    A. cyanide gas   B. hydrogen sulfide
    C. ozone   D. carbon monoxide
    E. hydrogen fluoride

21.＿＿＿

22. If the circulation of the hand becomes impaired due to use of a vibrating tool, what color will the injured area become when exposed to cold?

    A. White   B. Blue
    C. Red   D. Yellow
    E. Purple

22.＿＿＿

23. When the material from a volatilized solid condenses in cool air, _____ are formed.

    23.____

    A. aerosols   B. fumes
    C. mists   D. vapors
    E. gases

24. The two main professional disciplines of an occupational health program are

    24.____

        I.   industrial hygienist
       II. industrial toxicologist
     III. physician
     IV. health physicist
      V. industrial nurse

The CORRECT answer is:

    A. I, II   B. I, III
    C. I, IV   D. II, V
    E. I, V

25. The goal of an occupational health program is to

    25.____

    A. recognize health hazards in the work environment
    B. eliminate toxic materials from the work environment
    C. control air contaminants
    D. maintain and promote employee health
    E. ensure the efficiency of the work force

KEY (CORRECT ANSWERS)

1.	E		11.	C
2.	D		12.	D
3.	E		13.	A
4.	B		14.	A
5.	D		15.	C
6.	E		16.	B
7.	E		17.	E
8.	A		18.	E
9.	A		19.	A
10.	D		20.	B

21.	E
22.	A
23.	B
24.	B
25.	D

TEST 2

DIRECTIONS: Each question or incomplete statement is followed by several suggested answers or completions. Select the one that BEST answers the question or completes the statement. *PRINT THE LETTER OF THE CORRECT ANSWER IN THE SPACE AT THE RIGHT.*

1. All of the following are physical hazards EXCEPT

    A. electromagnetic and ionizing radiations
    B. noise
    C. tools and work areas
    D. vibration
    E. temperature

1._____

2. Hydrogen cyanide may produce

    A. narcosis   B. toxemia
    C. anesthesia   D. asphyxia
    E. paralysis

2._____

3. Many industrial materials that are normally inert may become toxic by

    A. chemical decomposition   B. dehydration
    C. freezing   D. sublimation
    E. condensation

3._____

4. A chemical substance which may be more readily absorbed into the red blood cells than oxygen and result in oxygen deficiency in the brain is

    A. carbon dioxide   B. nitrous oxide
    C. carbon monoxide   D. ammonia
    E. argon

4._____

5. Materials which react violently with water, decompose readily, or may cause fire on contact with combustible materials are defined as

    A. reducing agents   B. oxidents
    C. explosives   D. corrosives
    E. toxic

5._____

6. The rate of heat loss from the body by radiation and convection is determined by

    A. absolute temperature of the air
    B. wind velocity
    C. thermal gradient between skin and environment
    D. relative humidity
    E. pulse rate

6._____

7. The MOST commonly used dosimeter is the

    A. geiger counter   B. scintillation counter
    C. film badge   D. cloud chamber
    E. magnetometer

7._____

8. The task of designing equipment to best fit the human anatomy falls to   8._____

    A. physiotherapy   B. industrial medicine
    C. biomechanics   D. human engineering
    E. quantum mechanics

9. An oxygen concentration below which the individual may become *dizzy* and suffer rapid   9._____
heart beat and headache is

    A. 12%   B. 5%   C. 30%   D. 16%   E. 21%

10. Concentrations of airborne substances below which irritation or tissue damage may   10._____
result are called

    A. T.L.V.   B. M.L.D.
    C. T.I.S.   D. E.E.L.
    E. T.W.A.

11. "Core" temperature is measured   11._____

    A. at the center of the work area
    B. deep inside the body
    C. on the skin
    D. at body extremities
    E. at pulse points

12. An employee's body core temperature should not exceed   12._____

    A. 99° F.   B. 40° C.
    C. 98.6° F.   D. 100.4° F.
    E. 24.4° C.

13. Solvents and detergents are harmful to the skin because they   13._____

    A. do not readily evaporate
    B. combine with water to form toxic substances
    C. increase susceptibility to chemicals that do not ordinarily affect the skin
    D. are readily absorbed by the skin
    E. cause dehydration in the outer layers of the skin

14. Which of the following are good guidelines to safe lifting?   14._____
      I. Feet parted
     II. Back vertical
     III. Chin jutted forward
     IV. Grip with fingers, not palms
     V. Tuck elbows and arms in close to body
The CORRECT answer is:

    A. I, II, III, V   B. I, II, IV
    C. I, IV, V   D. I, V
    E. all of the above

15. What type of matter is *usually* produced when using oil during cutting and grinding oper-   15.____
    ations?

    A. Vapor   B. Dust
    C. Mist   D. Aerosol
    E. Gas

16. The extent of an employer's industrial health program depends *mainly* on   16.____

    A. health hazards in the work environment
    B. the manufacturing operations of the company
    C. the general healthfulness of the environment
    D. the employee response to the work environment
    E. identification of hazardous materials present in the work environment

17. The responsibility for promulgating and enforcing occupational and health standards   17.____
    belongs to the Department of

    A. Health and Human Services
    B. Labor
    C. Commerce
    D. the Interior
    E. Education

18. Engineering and biomechanical principles are required to eliminate _____ hazards.   18.____

    A. chemical   B. ergonomic
    C. environmental   D. physical
    E. biological

19. The tissues likely to be MOST affected by solvent vapors are   19.____

    A. cardiac muscle tissue
    B. the lining of the lungs
    C. endodermo layer of the skin
    D. lipid storage cells
    E. mucous membranes

20. Skin contact with chemical irritants may result in a skin condition called   20.____

    A. eczema   B. dermatitis
    C. shingles   D. edema
    E. cystitis

21. A dangerous material would NOT be   21.____

    A. explosive   B. corrosive
    C. flammable   D. soluble
    E. toxic

22. A health hazard exists when the range of temperature change from the "core tempera-   22.____
    ture" EXCEEDS _____ ° F.

    A. 10   B. 32   C. 5   D. 15   E. 25

23. Ionizing radiation causes damage to tissue *primarily* by   23._____

    A. disrupting the orbital electrons in the compounds of the body
    B. causing oxidation of amino acids
    C. producing caustic chemicals in the blood
    D. interfering with electromagnetic transmissions of the nerves
    E. causing hydrolysis of cell material

24. One of the MOST common sources of ultraviolet radiation in industry is   24._____

    A. fluorescent lighting   B. incandescent lighting
    C. heat lamps   D. microwave apparatus
    E. arc welding

25. Contaminants may exist as   25._____

    I. gas
    II. dust
    III. fume
    IV. mist
    V. vapor

The CORRECT answer is:

    A. I, III   B. I, III, V
    C. II, IV   D. II, V
    E. all of the above

KEY (CORRECT ANSWERS)

1.	C	11.	B
2.	D	12.	D
3.	A	13.	B
4.	C	14.	D
5.	B	15.	C
6.	C	16.	A
7.	C	17.	B
8.	C	18.	B
9.	D	19.	D
10.	A	20.	B

21.	D
22.	C
23.	A
24.	E
25.	E

TEST 3

DIRECTIONS: Each question or incomplete statement is followed by several suggested answers or completions. Select the one that BEST answers the question or completes the statement. *PRINT THE LETTER OF THE CORRECT ANSWER IN THE SPACE AT THE RIGHT.*

1. The body attempts to counteract the effects of high temperature by   1._____

   A. contracting the capillaries in the skin
   B. decreasing the rate of respiration
   C. increasing the heart beat rate
   D. ventilating; the alveoli
   E. lowering its "core" temperature

2. The theoretical freezing point of the skin is   2._____

   A. 0° F.   B. 14° C.   C. 30° F.   D. 55° F.   E. -10° C.

3. The organ MOST vulnerable to injury induced by laser energy is the   3._____

   A. skin   B. lungs
   C. brain   D. eyes
   E. intestines

4. Brucellosis is an occupational ailment of   4._____

   A. miners   B. printers
   C. stone cutters   D. farmers
   E. grain handlers

5. Formless fluids that expand to occupy the space in which they are confined are   5._____

   A. mists   B. aerosols
   C. vapors   D. smoke
   E. gases

6. The extent to which inhalation of harmful materials may irritate the respiratory system is determined by the   6._____

   A. solubility of the material
   B. ambient temperature of the material
   C. partial pressure of oxygen
   D. stress on the body at the time of inhalation
   E. relative humidity of the air containing the pollutant material

7. The BROADEST scope used to define an occupational health hazard is that it   7._____

   A. causes legally compensable illness
   B. impairs the health of employees enough to make them lose time from work
   C. impairs the health of employees enough to make them work at less than full efficiency
   D. is caused by a violation of Federal regulations
   E. causes an occupational disease

8. Primary irritation dermatitis and sensitization dermatitis are produced by   8.____

    A.   heat   B.   cold
    C.   formaldehyde   D.   alcohol
    E.   all of the above

9. All of the following are biological hazards EXCEPT   9.____

    A.   insects
    B.   personal cleanliness
    C.   electromagnetic and ionizing radiations
    D.   removal of industrial waste
    E.   bacterial contamination

10. Which of the following is NOT a solvent?   10.____

    A.   Chlorinated hydrocarbon
    B.   Aldehyde
    C.   Ketone
    D.   Carbon disulfide
    E.   Hydrogen peroxide

11. The "core" temperature of the body by mouth is   11.____

    A. 100° F.   B. 37° C.
    C. 212° F.   D. 96.8° F.
    E. 92° F.

12. The type of radial activity that is NOT of concern to the industrial hygienist is   12.____

    A.   alpha   B.   beta
    C.   neutron   D.   x-ray
    E.   gamma

13. Damage resulting from expansion or contraction of gas spaces within or adjacent to the   13.____
body is called

    A.   hyperventilation   B.   pulmonary edema
    C.   hypoxia   D.   barotrauma
    E.   implosion

14. Oxygen deficient atmospheres are most hazardous to the _____ system.   14.____

    A.   circulatory   B.   respiratory
    C.   nervous   D.   muscular
    E.   skeletal

15. Asbestos, a widely publicized environmental contaminant, belongs in the category of   15.____

    A.   gases   B.   vapors
    C.   aerosols   D.   smoke
    E.   dust

16. Which is NOT an example of a causative factor in primary irritation dermatitis?   16.____

    A. Heat   B. Acid
    C. Alkali   D. Pollen
    E. Cold

17. The radioactive particles *generally* considered to be an internal hazard are   17.____
        I.   alpha
       II. beta
      III. gamma
      IV. neutron
       V. x-ray
The CORRECT answer is:

    A. I, II   B. I, II, III
    C. III, IV   D. III, IV, V
    E. all of the above

18. Pressure differentials frequently affect the   18.____
        I.   eyes
       II. teeth
      III. sinuses
      IV. ears
       V. lungs
The CORRECT answer is:

    A. I, II, IV, V   B. I, IV, V
    C. II, III   D. II, III, IV
    E. III, IV, V

19. The finger BEST suited for operating mechanisms is the   19.____

    A. thumb   B. index finger
    C. middle finger   D. ring finger
    E. little finger

20. In order to penetrate to the alveoli of the lungs, dust particles must be smaller than   20.____
_____ micrometer.

    A. 1   B. 2-3   C. 5   D. 7   E. 10

21. The process by which a liquid is changed into the vapor state is   21.____

    A. evaporation   B. sublimation
    C. condensation   D. vaporization
    E. evacuation

22. The partial pressure of oxygen at the alveolar surface determines   22.____

    A. the rate of oxygen diffusion through the moist lung tissue membranes
    B. the percent of oxygen inhaled air
    C. the partial pressure of carbon dioxide in the blood stream
    D. whether or not dust particles will be retained in the lungs
    E. the hemoglobin levels of the erythrocytes

23. A condition where the body is unable to cool itself sufficiently, body temperature rises rapidly, and perspiration may cease, is called   23._____

    A. sunstroke   B. heat cramps
    C. heat exhaustion   D. thermal shock
    E. heat stroke

24. Ear damage in workers exposed to high air pressure environments *usually* results from   24._____

    A. poor worker hygiene
    B. greater rate of bacterial action under influence of higher air pressure
    C. fluid-filled sinuses
    D. blocked eustachian tubes
    E. all of the above

25. Normal sea level air contains *approximately* _____ percent oxygen.   25._____

    A. 21   B. 27   C. 32   D. 47   E. 55

KEY (CORRECT ANSWERS)

1. C	11. B		
2. C	12. C		
3. D	13. D		
4. D	14. C		
5. E	15. C		
6. A	16. D		
7. C	17. A		
8. C	18. D		
9. C	19. C		
10. E	20. C		

21. A
22. A
23. E
24. D
25. A

EXAMINATION SECTION
TEST 1

DIRECTIONS: Each question or incomplete statement is followed by several suggested answers or completions. Select the one that BEST answers the question or completes the statement. *PRINT THE LETTER OF THE CORRECT ANSWER IN THE SPACE AT THE RIGHT.*

1. Mucus   1._____
   - I.   gives up heat and moisture to air
   - II. contains antigen antibodies to combat disease
   - III. traps bacteria
   - IV. plays a role in ingestion of vital nutrients for cells
   - V.   dilutes irritating substances in the air

   The CORRECT answer is:
   - A. I, II, III   B. I, III, V
   - C. I, IV, V   D. II, III
   - E. II, III, IV

2. The passageway for air between the pharynx and the trachea is called the   2._____
   - A. larynx   B. nasopharynx
   - C. soft palate   D. laryngopharynx
   - E. esophagus

3. The common name of the larynx is the   3._____
   - A. food canal   B. windpipe
   - C. voice box   D. vocal cords
   - E. lung

4. Immediately behind the trachea is the   4._____
   - A. pharynx   B. esophagus
   - C. bronchus   D. lungs
   - E. larynx

5. A loud voice is due to   5._____
   - A. greater force and amount of air expelled from the lungs
   - B. longer vocal cords
   - C. greater vocal cord tension
   - D. larger lungs
   - E. larger larynx

6. The lungs are covered by a membrane called the   6._____
   - A. mesyntary   B. pericardium
   - C. omentum   D. pleura
   - E. dura

7. The lung surface clings to the chest wall because of the   7._____
   - A. negative pressure of the intrapleural space
   - B. mucus lining of the pleural cavity

C. fibrous connective tissue
D. interstitial cohesion
E. contraction of smooth muscle in the pleural lining

8. Incomplete expansion of the lungs is termed   8.____

    A. dyspnea   B. pulmonary edema
    C. thoraxemia   D. atelectasis
    E. pneumonia

9. An outpouring of fluid in the lungs in response to irritation produces   9.____

    A. bronchitis   B. pneumonitis
    C. rhinitis   D. baritosis
    E. keratitis

10. The movement of gaseous molecules from an area of high concentration to an area of   10.____
low concentration is called

    A. metamorphosis   B. metabolism
    C. diffusion   D. osmosis
    E. dispersion

11. The inhalation of air is accomplished by the muscles of the ribs or intercostals and the 11.____

    A. diaphragm   B. abdominal muscles
    C. muscles of the lungs   D. pulmonary muscles
    E. pectoral muscles

12. Procedures useful in evaluating impairments of the respiratory system include all of the   12.____
following EXCEPT

    A. electrocardiogram
    B. hematocrit
    C. chest roentgenography
    D. complete medical history
    E. C.A.T. Scan

13. Results of tests for ventilatory function should be expressed in terms of   13.____

    A. foot pounds per second
    B. quarts per minutes
    C. cubic inches per minute
    D. liters per minute
    E. cubic feet per second

14. The respiratory system presents a quick and direct avenue of entry for toxic materials   14.____
because of

    A. its direct contact with the environment
    B. the great amounts of surface area involved
    C. the average person's breath per minute
    D. the thin tissues involved in respiration
    E. its intimate association with the circulatory system

15. How many pairs of ribs surround and guard the lungs?   15.____

    A. 7   B. 10   C. 6   D. 8   E. 12

16. Vital Capacity is the sum of   16.____
        I.   tidal volume
       II. inspiratory reserve volume
      III. forced vital capacity
      IV. expiratory reserve volume
       V. total lung capacity
The CORRECT answer is:

    A. I, II, IV   B. I, V
    C. II, III, IV   D. II, IV
    E. II, IV, V

17. Guarding the opening to the trachea is a thin leaf-shaped valve called the   17.____

    A. uvula   B. pyloris
    C. mitral valve   D. semi lunar valve
    E. epiglottis

18. The MOST important system of the human body to the industrial hygienist is the   18.____
        _____ system.

    A. circulatory   B. nervous
    C. muscular   D. respiratory
    E. skeletal

19. Respiration begins with the   19.____

    A. mouth   B. nose
    C. lungs   D. trachea
    E. pharynx

20. Air moves from the nasal cavity into the   20.____

    A. trachea   B. larynx
    C. bronchus   D. pharynx
    E. lungs

21. Voice sounds are caused by   21.____

    A. air trapped in the voice box
    B. the tongue and muscles of the mouth
    C. incoming air passing through the voice box
    D. air expelled from the lungs
    E. vibration of the epiglottis

22. The mediastinum is   22.____

    A. a cluster of air sacs
    B. the space between the two pleural layers
    C. the site where the trachea divides
    D. the narrow partition that divides the nose
    E. the space between the left and right lung

23. The tiny air sacs of the lungs are

    A. bronchiole   B. alveoli
    C. hephrons   D. bursa
    E. villi

23.____

24. A partial collapse of the lung may be caused by

    A. hypertrophy of the bronchioles
    B. occlusion of a bronchus
    C. contraction of the bronchial tubes
    D. constriction of the tube muscles
    E. negative pressure of the intrapleural space

24.____

25. Dusty lungs, the result of continued inhalation of various kinds of dusts, is called

    A. pneumonitis   B. polyeythemia
    C. pneumoconiosis   D. pterygium
    E. siderosis

25.____

KEY (CORRECT ANSWERS)

1. B		11. A
2. A		12. E
3. C		13. D
4. B		14. E
5. A		15. E
6. D		16. A
7. A		17. E
8. D		18. D
9. B		19. B
10. C		20. D

21.	D
22.	E
23.	B
24.	B
25.	C

TEST 2

DIRECTIONS: Each question or incomplete statement is followed by several suggested answers or completions. Select the one that BEST answers the question or completes the statement. *PRINT THE LETTER OF THE CORRECT ANSWER IN THE SPACE AT THE RIGHT.*

1. Hemoglobin molecules that have lost their oxygen are called _____ hemoglobin.   1.___

    A. reduced   B. hypo
    C. empty   D. negative
    E. nor

2. The automatic regulation of breathing is accomplished by the   2.___

    A. cerebrum   B. cerebellum
    C. medulla   D. hypothalmus
    E. gray matter

3. The medical term for shortness of breath is   3.___

    A. bronchitis   B. pneumothorax
    C. dyspnea   D. hyperventilation
    E. asthma

4. Forced expiratory volume ("FEV") and forced vital capacity ("FVC") tests should be administered   4.___

    A. only once due to the strenuous nature of the test
    B. 5 times, taking an average
    C. 3 times, taking the best result
    D. 2 times, taking the lowest reading
    E. 4 times, taking the average

5. All of the following air contaminants may produce pulmonary edema EXCEPT   5.___

    A. hydrogen fluoride   B. nitrogen dioxide
    C. phosgene   D. ozone
    E. sulfur dioxide

6. The floor of the chest cavity is formed by the   6.___

    A. stomach   B. hepar
    C. diaphragm   D. colon
    E. sternum

7. The vital lung capacity of a healthy person decreases with age due to a(n)   7.___

    A. decrease in the elasticity of tissues
    B. decrease in the area of surfaces where gas exchange takes place
    C. increase of fluid in the lungs
    D. increase of fibrotic tissue in the alveolar sacs
    E. narrowing of the bronchioles

8. The triangular box composed of nine cartilages, joined together by ligaments, and controlled by skeletal muscle is called the   8.___

    A. trachea   B. pharynx
    C. larynx   D. esophagus
    E. epiglottis

9. All living cells of the body are engaged in a series of chemical processes. The name given to the sum total of these processes is

    A. physiology
    C. catabolism
    E. metabolism

    B. anabolism
    D. mytosis

9.____

10. The lungs have good defenses against particulates. When unimpaired, these clearance mechanisms remove _____ percent of the insoluble dust deposited in the lungs.

    A. 85   B. 75   C. 90   D. 99   E. 94

10.____

11. When sizable liquid or solid particles come in contact with the glottis, the

    A. epiglottis opens
    C. person hiccups
    E. larynx opens

    B. person coughs
    D. person vomits

11.____

12. The common name of the trachea is the

    A. food channel
    C. valve
    E. windpipe

    B. nasal passage
    D. throat

12.____

13. The pleural membranes are prevented from rubbing against each other during breathing by

    A. a layer of air
    C. tiny cartilages
    E. hairlike cilia

    B. a layer of fluid
    D. fibrous tissue

13.____

14. Which of the following represents the most extensive and intimate contact of the body with the ambient atmosphere?

    A. Circulatory system
    B. Hair
    C. Lungs
    D. Infrastructure of the kidneys
    E. Skin

14.____

15. Pleurisy is caused by

    A. inflammation of the pleurae's mucous membrane
    B. loss of the pleurae's lubricating properties
    C. hypertrophy of the pleura
    D. introduction of a layer of fluid between the pleurae
    E. introduction of air between the pleural layers

15.____

16. The smallest particles of dust will likely be deposited in the

    A. trachea
    B. alveoli spaces
    C. nasal passages
    D. upper respiratory tubes
    E. bronchial tubes

16.____

17. In the *majority* of people, during routine activities, breathing is regulated by

    A. lack of oxygen
    B. negative pressure in the lungs
    C. the maintenance of carbon dioxide in the blood
    D. biorhythms
    E. a need to regulate body temperature

17.____

18. The ventilation capacity of the lungs may be measured with an instrument called a

    A. breathometer   B. pulmomonometer
    C. breathylizer   D. barograph
    E. spirometer

18.____

19. An example of decreased breathing capacity due to restriction is

    A. air or fluid in the pleural space
    B. bronchitis
    C. emphysema
    D. asthma
    E. pneumonia

19.____

20. The decreased oxygen-carrying capacity of the blood is often termed

    A. hypoxemia   B. narcosis
    C. cyanosis   D. carboxia
    E. emphysema

20.____

21. The nose is divided into right and left nasal cavities by the

    A. soft palate   B. xyphoid process
    C. lacrimal ridge   D. septum
    E. diverticulum

21.____

22. Intrapulmonic pressure is below atmospheric pressure

    A. at the end of expiration
    B. during inspiration
    C. at the end of inspiration
    D. during expiration
    E. at no time

22.____

23. The MOST common form of decreased breathing capacity is

    A. increased resistance to the flow of air
    B. circulatory impairment
    C. decreased oxygen carrying capacity of the blood
    D. pulmonary resection
    E. stress

23.____

24. Some cells of the body are more dependent on a constant oxygen supply than others   24.____
because they

    A. are larger
    B. require more energy
    C. have a specialized function
    D. die and cannot be reproduced
    E. contain nerve filaments

25. The function of the turbinates is to   25.____

    A. condition the air
    B. trap dust particles
    C. relay information on odors
    D. moisten air
    E. remove particles

KEY (CORRECT ANSWERS)

1.	A	11.	B
2.	C	12.	E
3.	C	13.	B
4.	C	14.	C
5.	E	15.	B
6.	C	16.	B
7.	A	17.	C
8.	C	18.	E
9.	E	19.	A
10.	D	20.	A

21.	D
22.	B
23.	A
24.	D
25.	A

TEST 3

DIRECTIONS: Each question or incomplete statement is followed by several suggested answers or completions. Select the one that BEST answers the question or completes the statement. *PRINT THE LETTER OF THE CORRECT ANSWER IN THE SPACE AT THE RIGHT.*

1. The scroll-like bones on both sides of the septum are called

   A. turbinates
   C. adenoids
   E. pleura
   B. alveoli
   D. bronchiole

   1._____

2. The *approximate* length of the trachea is

   A. 4 1/2 inches
   C. 3.2 cm
   E. 2.54 cm
   B. 8 inches
   D. 1 foot

   2._____

3. The respiratory system includes all of the following EXCEPT the

   A. diaphragm
   C. esophagus
   E. bronchi
   B. mouth
   D. larynx

   3._____

4. The common name of the pharynx is the

   A. vocal cords
   C. windpipe
   E. throat
   B. nasal passages
   D. voice box

   4._____

5. The right and left bronchi are divisions of the

   A. trachea
   C. nasopharynx
   E. esophagus
   B. pharynx
   D. collarbone

   5._____

6. Most aspirated materials enter the right lung because the
   I. right main stem bronchus is wider
   II. right main stem bronchus is shorter
   III. direction of the right main stem bronchus is almost identical with that of the trachea
   IV. right lung has fewer lobes
   V. right main stem bronchus is stiffened by rings of cartilage
   The CORRECT answer is:

   A. I, II, III
   C. I, IV, V
   E. II, IV, V
   B. I, II, IV
   D. II, III, V

   6._____

7. Constriction of the tube muscles in response to irritation is called

   A. emphysema
   C. rhinitis
   E. sinusitus
   B. allergy
   D. asthma

   7._____

8. Inflammation of the mucous membrane of the nasal passages is called 8.____

   A. laryngitis
   C. occlusion
   E. rhinitis
   B. sinusitis
   D. mucosa

9. An infection involving a lobe on the lung is known as 9.____

   A. tuberculosis
   C. emphysema
   E. pneumonia
   B. atelectasis
   D. pleurisy

10. The process that involves a chemical change is 10.____

    A. breathing
    C. internal respiration
    E. true respiration
    B. external respiration
    D. diffusion

11. Hemoglobin, the oxygen-carrying pigment of the blood, is a molecule made up of protein 11.____
    and

    A. copper
    C. an enzyme
    E. melanin
    B. iron
    D. amino acid

12. A negative pressure is defined as any pressure below atmospheric pressure, which at 12.____
    sea level is _____ mm of mercury.

    A. 100   B. 1540   C. 71   D. 760   E. 88

13. The pressure of air within the bronchial tree and alveoli is referred to as _____ pres- 13.____
    sure.

    A. ambient
    C. internal
    E. intrapulmonic
    B. respiratory
    D. bronchial

14. Aerosols that are NOT removed from the alveoli by capillary action may be removed by 14.____

    A. phagocytic cells
    C. the blood stream
    E. the cough mechanism
    B. cilia
    D. antibodies

15. The degree of dysfunction of the respiratory system is often difficult to evaluate because 15.____
    of

    I. disease of other systems such as cardiovascular
    II. large pulmonary reserves normally present
    III. patient's emotional response to disease or injury
    IV. socioeconomic background of the patient
    V. lack of accurate diagnostic tools
    The CORRECT answer is:

    A. I, II, III
    C. I, III, V
    E. II, III, IV
    B. I, III, IV
    D. I, IV, V

16. The possibility of reversal in cases of airway obstruction is indicated when the degree of improvement in F.E.V. after inhalation of a bronchodilater is *at least*

    A. 5%   B. 15%   C. 25%   D. 50%   E. 75%

16.____

17. An exercise test used to diagnose respiratory dysfunction in patients who have no apparent symptoms at rest is

    A. ten minute run in place
    B. isometric exercise
    C. Borden stress test
    D. Master's two-step test
    E. quarter mile fast walk

17.____

18. The forced expiratory volume divided by the forced vital capacity times 100 of a healthy person should EXCEED

    A. 90%   B. 70%   C. 50%   D. 95%   E. 33%

18.____

19. The interpretation of damage to the respiratory system is aided by the use of the AMA's

    A. Medical Technicians Guide to Lung Dysfunction
    B. Diagnostic Techniques for Lung Disorders
    C. Handbook of Medical Evaluative Techniques
    D. Text of Pulmonary Dysfunctions
    E. Guide to Evaluation of Permanent Impairment

19.____

20. The nasal cavities are open to the outside through the

    A. vestibules
    C. anterior nares
    E. the posterior septums
    B. venules
    D. the superior vomers

20.____

21. The interior walls of the nose are covered with _____ membranes.

    A. mucous
    C. sinal
    E. elastic
    B. vestibular
    D. arachnoid

21.____

22. The millions of cilia lining the nasal cavity

    A. help the mucus clean the incoming air
    B. are the stimulus for inspiration
    C. are the stimulus for expiration
    D. relay information on odors to the olfactory nerve
    E. make it possible to breathe with comfort when the passages are blocked

22.____

23. What can trigger breathing action?

    A. An increase in the oxygen level of the blood
    B. An increase of pressure within the chest
    C. Intrapulmonic pressure rising above atmospheric pressure
    D. An increase of the carbon dioxide level of the blood
    E. Negative atmospheric pressure in the intrapleural space

23.____

24. A person breathes in and out _____ times a minute while in a relaxed state.   24._____

    A. 4-6   B. 10-14
    C. 20-24   D. 36-40
    E. 75-80

25. The volume of gas inspired or expired during each respiratory cycle is   25._____

    A. total lung capacity
    B. vital capacity
    C. tidal volume
    D. functional residual capacity
    E. residual volume

KEY (CORRECT ANSWERS)

1.	A		11.	B
2.	A		12.	D
3.	C		13.	E
4.	E		14.	A
5.	A		15.	A
6.	A		16.	B
7.	D		17.	D
8.	E		18.	B
9.	E		19.	E
10.	E		20.	C

21.	A
22.	A
23.	D
24.	B
25.	C

Made in the USA
Columbia, SC
26 March 2023

14347434R00083